THE
SECRET
PRINCIPLES
OF
GENIUS

I. C. ROBLEDO

JAICO PUBLISHING HOUSE

Ahmedabad Bangalore Bhopal Chennai
Delhi Hyderabad Kolkata Lucknow Mumbai

Published by Jaico Publishing House
A-2 Jash Chambers, 7-A Sir Phirozshah Mehta Road
Fort, Mumbai - 400 001
jaicopub@jaicobooks.com
www.jaicobooks.com

Published in arrangement with
Issac Robledo
PO Box 351254, Palm Coast
FL 32135-1254, USA

THE SECRET PRINCIPLES OF GENIUS
ISBN 978-93-86867-78-0

First Jaico Impression: 2018
Second Jaico Impression: 2020

Printed by
Pashupati Printers, Delhi

Contents

Introduction

Why I Wrote This Book

The idea for this book has been on my mind for quite a long time. I've had an interest in the minds, abilities, and lives of geniuses for many, many years. I used to think the genius mind must process information so much faster than normal. I believed those people who were geniuses must have had an easy life with a mind so powerful. I also believed the accomplishments of many geniuses would have been impossible for anyone else. This was naïve, as since then I have found this thinking to be misguided. I have learned a great deal through my investigations of brilliant minds, and I want to share that with you. I assure you this will be an eye-opening experience.

Briefly, I want to share with you how I first started learning about genius minds, and how I became fascinated with the topic. I studied psychology at Purdue University in Indiana. While I was there, I often went to the Hicks Undergraduate Library in between classes. Once, I was browsing through the books on the shelves, and one called *Terman's Kids: The Groundbreaking Study of How the Gifted Grow Up* caught my attention. It was about a longitudinal study, examining the lives of many gifted students, reporting on their accomplishments as they grew up. I quickly finished the book, and the insightful details in it made me want to learn even more. This book was really just the beginning. I have since read many other formal studies, books, and a wide range of sources on intelligence, genius, and giftedness.

After I had read many books and absorbed a great deal of information about brilliant people, I started to wonder if there were principles of genius anyone could learn and apply. However, I never found a book quite like the one I was looking for. There wasn't one that clearly stated principles many geniuses through history have used, in a way that could be easily understood and applied. I knew these principles existed, but it was as if they were secret, or hidden away, waiting to be discovered. This motivated me to delve deeper, investigating what these principles may be, and ultimately compiling them into this book. In the end, I believe this will be a helpful resource to learning how geniuses think and work, and to unleashing your own genius potential.

Why the Secret Principles Matter to Me

Growing up, I often had a sense that I wasn't using my mind to its full capability. I tended to do well enough at school or in any work I needed to do, but I knew I had more potential. It frustrated me that I didn't know how to use my mind to its full power. This feeling started when I was a child, but it persisted into my teens and even into my early adulthood. I felt that there had to be a better way to think, learn, and solve problems. I often felt stuck, trying to figure out the best way to think through a problem, but unable to make any progress. To make things more frustrating, I had no idea where to go for help with this.

For a while, I gave up. I gave up on improving myself, thinking there was no way to move forward. My mind stagnated, and I stopped moving forward with my goals. I was accumulating facts, but not truly learning, understanding, or advancing myself in any meaningful way. I fear this is common in society. We give up on ourselves too easily. This sort of thing tends to happen when we're young, naïve and fragile, because we don't know any better.

When I had given up, I sometimes felt completely lost both in school and life, like I didn't truly know or understand anything deeply. I was able to earn decent grades without understanding the material, which seemed backward and strange to me. But this became a terrible pattern, which made me feel less and less intelligent, as my grades showed that I understood things which I really did not. Luckily, after years of no real progress in my abilities, I decided my life was headed in the wrong direction. So I dedicated myself to solving the problem. But the first question was "*What is the problem?*" Ultimately, I realized that I needed principles to follow which would set my mind on a better path. My mind felt untrained, unfocused, and even unintelligent. But I had a sense that I was not truly unintelligent. I just needed to train my mind to work better and get it focused again. This would help me to feel and act more intelligently. I would be more confident too, and as a result I would never give up on myself again.

And so I set out to discover what these principles could be...

What the Secret Principles of Genius Can Do for You

I want you to think about what intelligence is for a moment. Intelligence is usually thought of as something that happens in the mind. But intelligence is also a behavior. Intelligence manifests itself through actions we take. Rather than focus on the intelligent thoughts that lead to intelligent behaviors, what if we could flip this around? What if we could focus on the intelligent behaviors that lead to intelligent thoughts? Of course, some of this book does focus on thoughts, but the main focus is on concrete actions we can take to lead intelligent lives. Whether you think you are very smart, or not as smart as you would like to be, I believe *The Secret Principles of Genius* will help you in building a peak performing mind.

One of the big motivations for me to write this book was that I didn't want anyone to give up on themselves, like I once did. Giving up is the worst thing you can do. When you give up, you stop seeing possibilities and opportunities. Everything becomes clouded in darkness. You will feel that you are not especially intelligent, but you will blame it on yourself, probably on your genetics or laziness. But the truth is if you keep an open mind, allow yourself to wake up to reality, and apply the principles in this book, you can start on your own path to genius. No one can stop you if you choose to move in that direction. But if you give up, no one will be able to help you either.

Even if you are fully confident in your abilities, and you

aren't sure if this book is for you, I want you to consider this. If everything goes well in our childhood, then our families, parents, and educators will do everything they can to prepare us for the future. They often mean the best, and do everything in their power to show us the proper path. This involves the proper way to lead our lives, the way to success, and so forth. But there is something missing... I get a mental image here of a baby bird, up sky high in a nest somewhere. Sooner or later, you find yourself in the position of this bird. You feel unprepared, looking down at a hundred feet of air between you and the ground. You look at your tiny wings, and they don't seem strong or big enough yet. You decide it's best to wait for another day to fly. But wait a minute! Something bumps you from behind (maybe the wind, or even your mother) and you go shooting down fast toward the ground. You flap your wings so hard that you didn't think it was possible. You're flying, you're falling, you're flying, and you're falling! Are you going to land safely? Are you going to hurt yourself terribly? Sooner or later, even as people, not birds, we will find ourselves in such situations. And we will feel completely unprepared, no matter what we were taught.

For example, you may find yourself in situations where you are uncertain what is happening, what to do, where to turn. *The Secret Principles of Genius* can help with this. You may feel that everything you thought you knew was wrong. You have to start from scratch and you aren't sure how to start over, abandoning everything you had learned. The principles can help with this. You may be faced with the most difficult problem of your life. It seems impossible and you can feel the weight of it heavy on your shoulders. The principles can help with this, too. But this isn't a manual to use when you have a specific overwhelming problem that needs to be taken care of right away. The greatest benefits come when the principles are applied on a daily basis. Then, when you find yourself deep in the unknown, possibly with no one to help you, you will be much better prepared to manage for yourself.

I am aware that the image of a baby bird falling from its nest can seem overly dramatic. Perhaps you have never experienced anything quite that unsettling. But life can be unpredictable. We don't know what challenges we will need to face in the future. In my young adulthood, I often felt lost and confused. Sometimes that feeling led to great stress, and at times I did feel like the falling bird, uncertain where I would end up. But when I began to discover the principles, this changed. I started to feel more in control of my life. I started to have a better understanding of people and the world. The road to progress became much clearer. The feelings of being lost started to fade away.

My point is if you find this book at the right time, you can use it to transform your life. I have used the contents of it to transform my own, so I know it can be done. I know you can do it.

What Does it Mean to Be a Genius?

If you have ever known a brilliant person, they make certain things look easy and natural. In their presence, you may get the sense that what they do really isn't so tough. Maybe with a bit of time and effort you too could have painted the *Mona Lisa*. But the truth is they put a great deal of work in to attain that level of ability. Here is a quick story to show you what I mean.

Legend has it that Pablo Picasso, the famous artist, was sitting in a Paris café when a gentleman came to him and asked if he could do a quick drawing on a napkin. Picasso politely agreed. Quickly and seemingly without effort, he made the drawing, and was about to hand back the napkin — but first he asked for a huge amount of money. The gentleman was shocked: "Why would you ask for so much? It only took you a minute to draw this!" "No", Picasso said, "It took me 40 years."

Picasso was cleverly showing that just because he created masterful work on a napkin, made it look easy, and did it fast, doesn't mean it was always this way. It took him 40 years of hard work to get that good.

Genius often appears to occur instantly, automatically, or effortlessly, but the truth is that it is the furthest thing from this. We all wish these things were true, but wishing it, rather than abiding by the principles and doing the work required, is what will prevent most of us from advancing our intellect to a higher level. Understand that the outcomes of genius may appear easy, but the process to get there is not.

How can we define genius? To me, a genius is someone with a brilliant mind who has had great accomplishments in a challenging field, and changed the world in some meaningful way. As vague as this definition may seem, the essence of genius is limitless. There appear to be no bounds to what geniuses can accomplish. To define it much further, is to limit something that is supposed to be limitless. Keep in mind that geniuses can occur in virtually any field – it could be music, art, science, math, literature, architecture, or something else. You may think you would know when you are in its presence, but perhaps not. Often times, the genius is only understood by another one, or by at least someone who is an expert in the same field. For example, if you only know basic math, a genius who is solving the most difficult problems in the field will go unnoticed.

There is another perspective I would like to offer, which everyone may not agree with. Genius is defined not just by outcomes, such as a masterful work of architecture or a brilliant solution to a math problem no one has been able to solve for years. It is also defined by the expectations we have for a specific entity. I say entity because we have different expectations for humans than for dogs or for the intelligence of computers (e.g., artificial intelligence). Likewise, we have different expectations for people with different backgrounds. We will not expect the same abilities from someone who lives with nature, away from society and technology (such as indigenous tribes of Papua, New Guinea) as we would from an artist living in New York City. The former is more likely to have excellent survival skills in the wild, and the latter is more likely to be familiar with art and culture.

As a last point, in case you are not convinced, consider computer intelligence. Do you think a computer is ingenious because it can calculate thousands of math operations in a second, while it would take you days or weeks to do the same thing? Probably not, because we expect it to be able to do such things. They have so much processing power that it is trivial for the computer to accomplish this. Yet the late Kim Peek, whose life inspired the movie *Rain Man* starring Tom Cruise and Dustin Hoffman, was considered a genius by many. He has actually been referred to as a mega-savant for his phenomenal abilities. For example, he had the ability to calculate *many times faster* than a human with a calculator could. And he was known to speed-read, with a perfect memory of what he had read. Peek had a rare disorder called FG Syndrome, but he also had a great gift, a genius ability to help compensate.

When defining genius, it's also important to realize this is a status that is never fully reached. Instead, it is something to aspire to. Your status of genius or non-genius is something that can be debated after your death, if people choose to. If they debate it during your life, consider it an honor. But to join the debate or try to convince people you are a genius is a waste of time. There can be danger and heartache in pursuing the path of genius just for the glory. They are not always well recognized for their efforts, or even understood. Genius isn't a status to reach, rather it is a journey to greatness. It is the aspiration and relentless pursuit of something greater than what you are at the present moment.

As the topic of genius comes up, you may wonder about IQ (Intelligence Quotient). Some people may be surprised at this, but you do not need a super high IQ to be a genius. The tests are usually centered on math, verbal, and abstract reasoning skills. They are unlikely to capture artistic genius or other forms of genius that fall outside these skill sets. Also, the tests aren't perfect, and people's skills and abilities are more complex than the tests can measure. Someone with an IQ that isn't very high may need to work harder, but I believe it is possible to attain a genius level accomplishment without the highest of IQ scores. Consider that many people with high IQs have not had special accomplishments. A high score alone will not be enough to reach a genius level. In the end, this isn't worth worrying about. Regardless of your score, if you tap into the principles of genius, you will tap further into your true potential.

The Importance of These Principles

If you are going to read this book, you probably want to know where these principles came from. My research into many geniuses throughout history has led me to discover them. I have read many books about great minds, including biographies, psychological studies, and gained information from a wide variety of resources, over many, many years. I estimate that I have read at least fifty books and hundreds of articles in the area of psychology, intelligence, genius, and learning.

Sometimes, I have also had the good fortune to be in the presence of brilliant minds. At those times I have paid attention to anything that could potentially be a principle of genius. The important thing for you is to know that every principle in this book has been researched, and found to occur in a variety of bright minds, through a range of time periods in history, and in many different contexts. These are the universal principles of genius.

I have been searching for these principles for many years. I had a sense that they existed, and that if I kept searching, I would find them and understand them, and be able to show others how they could be put to good use. This search was a lot like looking for clues. In my research, rarely were broad principles discussed. Instead, it was usually detailed events. I needed to pay attention to the patterns and understand when I had come across a broader principle.

Are these ALL of the principles of genius? I am sure they aren't. But my goal was to identify the major principles that most geniuses have used. These principles can apply to a wide range of situations. They can apply to the artist, the scientist, the engineer, the writer, the inventor, and so forth. Also, I believe these are the most important and critical principles we can apply to make progress on our path toward genius.

Ultimately, these principles are important because the great geniuses of current and past times have used them. This includes people such as Socrates, Albert Einstein, Leonardo da Vinci, Isaac Newton, Charles Darwin, Johann Wolfgang von Goethe, Ludwig van Beethoven, Stephen Hawking, and many others. These are the brilliant minds whose principles I have uncovered from their writings, biographies, and the lives they lived.

You may wonder, if these principles are so important, why have they been kept secret? One of the reasons many of them have been hidden is not because these brilliant minds intended to keep them away from the public. Instead, it is more likely that they discovered some of the principles, noticed how effective they were and applied them through habit. Then in time these people may have credited their own brilliance with their successes, rather than a specific principle. It is also possible that some people may have assumed certain principles were obvious to everyone else even when that was not true. Also, many geniuses through history might not have realized how great of an impact the principles had on their accomplishments. We have the privilege of being able to look back on many of their lives, and seeing how specific principles led them to some of the greatest discoveries of all time. They did not. In any case, the secret principles which were before hidden, are now available to you for your personal benefit.

Unblock the Path to Genius

The goal of this book is to unblock the path toward genius for you. Up until now, it has been closed off because without knowing the principles geniuses have used throughout history, it is extremely difficult to make much progress. Just understand that all I can do is *unblock the path* and show you the way, but it is you who has to *put in the work* to get there.

The premise of this book is that perhaps we could all be geniuses if we just knew the right principles to apply, which are ordinarily hidden away from us. Of course, this doesn't mean it will be an easy road to get there. You may ask what you have to do to become a genius. Well, some of the best advice I have ever received in life is to focus on the things you can control. When it comes to the status of genius, you can either declare yourself one (and risk getting laughed at), or in time it is possible others will perceive you as a genius because of your accomplishments. The first option is not advised, and the second option (e.g., how others think of you) is out of your control.

Instead of focusing on those, I would recommend choosing the most relevant principles to your goals and life, and to put them into action. In doing so, you will become closer to the greatest minds in history. This will put you on the path to unlocking the true genius inside of you.

Before You Continue...

As a thank you for reading, I want you to have this free guide:

Step Up Your Learning: Free Tools to Learn Almost Anything
mentalmax.net/EN

Have you ever wondered what the best sites and resources for learning are? It takes time and effort to figure out which sites are worth it and which are not. I hope to save you some of that time so you can spend more of it learning instead of searching the Internet.

In the past ten years or so, there has been a free learning revolution happening. More and more resources for learning are becoming available to the public at no cost. With so many new ones coming out, it's easy to miss out on some of the great learning opportunities available. Fortunately for you, this guide is short at around 4,000 words, and tells you exactly what you need to know.

The guide stems from my own experiences of using a variety of learning sites and resources. In it, you will discover the best places to go for learning at no cost. Also, I'll explain which resources are best for you, depending on your learning goals.

You can download this free guide as a PDF by typing this website into your browser: mentalmax.net/EN

Now, let's get back on topic.

Personal Qualities
of Genius

"Everybody is a genius. But if you judge a fish by its ability to climb a tree, it will live its whole life believing that it is stupid."

— **Albert Einstein**, German-born theoretical physicist.

Geniuses tend to have certain personal qualities about them that start showing up even at a young age. They have specific tendencies that define them. These are things we may even attribute to their personalities. These qualities have an impact on their priorities, mindset, and the actions they choose to take. For example, geniuses tend to be curious (Principle #2), to pursue high levels of challenge (Principle #4), and to refuse to give up in the face of obstacles (Principle #8).

Personal qualities are important because we take them with us everywhere we go. These qualities are a deep part of who you are. Because of this, it doesn't feel like a choice to have them, but it is. You can decide to change and do something different at any time you wish. This section is meant to help you achieve this. It will be a matter of implementing new habits, routines, and patterns. By having the right personal qualities in your life, you will be able to maximize your effectiveness with the rest of the principles of this book.

Use Your Senses to Their Full Power

"The functions to be established by the child fall into two groups: (1) the motor functions by which he is to secure his balance and learn to walk, and to coordinate his movements; (2) the sensory functions through which, receiving sensations from his environment, he lays the foundations of his intelligence by a continual exercise of observation, comparison and judgment.

In this way he gradually comes to be acquainted with his environment and to develop his intelligence."

— **Maria Montessori,** Italian physician and educator best known for the philosophy of education that bears her name and her writing on scientific pedagogy.

Geniuses Who Applied the Principle

George Berkeley, Johann Wolfgang von Goethe, Edwin Hubble, David Hume, Helen Keller, John Locke, Maria Montessori, A research participant identified only as "S" (from A. R. Luria's *The Mind of a Mnemonist*), Nikola Tesla, Ben Underwood, Leonardo da Vinci.

Description of the Principle

Today, most of us are very visual, and we may have to be reminded that we have other senses we can use to experience the world. Of course, there is sight, smell, hearing, touch, and taste. As much as we use visual information, it is limiting if that is all we use. Realize that when you see a bird's feathers, you experience them one way. When you touch those feathers, you understand them on a much deeper level. They have texture, shape, and rigidity, for example.

As you know, we are surrounded by a massive amount of sensory stimulation every day. But every species, including humans, has limits as to what can be perceived. For example, humans usually cannot perceive infrared or ultraviolet light. We cannot perceive smells as sensitively as most species of dogs would. Also, we can't perceive sounds the way a bat does. A bat is able to 'see' with echolocation. It makes a sound, and can judge where objects are based on how the echoes come off of walls and any surrounding objects. Nonetheless, even with our limited abilities we are well-equipped to sense the world around us.

Our senses are easy to take for granted. The most interesting cases of how people use their senses actually come from those who did not have all of them. For example, Helen Keller was the first person to graduate college who was both deaf and blind. She began a path to greater understanding when her teacher, Anne Sullivan, ran Hellen's hand through water, and spelled out w-a-t-e-r onto the palm of her other hand at the same time. This was when Keller first realized that the feeling of running water in her hand could connect directly with the word "water".

Another curious case is of Ben Underwood. He had his eyes removed at three years old because of retinal cancer. What is so interesting about Underwood is that he started developing a system of echolocation for himself at a young age. He would make clicking noises, which helped him 'see' the world, more similarly to how a bat does with its ears than most humans do with their eyes. He could perform feats that seemed impossible for a blind boy, such as playing basketball, riding a bike, and skateboarding. Underwood's abilities were so phenomenal that he was the subject of the 2003 TV Series *Extraordinary People*, where investigators attempted to find the limits of his abilities. Ultimately, his resourcefulness even without eyesight reveals that most of us don't use our senses to their full capacity. Tragically, he passed away in 2009 at just 16 years old from a return of his cancer.

Since this book is about achieving a genius level in our pursuits, I think it is powerful to consider where Ben Underwood may have gotten his strength and motivation from, to develop his senses to a seemingly supernatural level. Clearly this had to be his mother, Aquanetta Gordon. She wrote this at BenUnderwood.com:

> *Ben awoke from the surgery [where they removed his eyes] and said "Mom I can't see anymore, I can't see anymore. Oh mom I can't see." After praying for strength and receiving from God, I said, "Ben YES YOU CAN SEE," and I took his little hands and put them on my face and said, "[Touch] me, you can see me with your hands," next, I put my hand to his nose and said, "Smell me, you can see me with your nose," then I said, "Hear me, you can see me with your ears. You can't use your eyes anymore, but you have your hands, your nose, and your ears." I tell this one thing, Ben has been seeing ever since.*

Rather than focus on the sense he no longer had, his mother immediately chose to focus on the senses the young Ben did have. Recall that he was only three years old at the time his eyes were removed. Yet she found a way to explain her feelings to him in a way that would not make him scared and worried. Instead, he would be empowered through her words, as we can see that he grew up doing all of the normal things other children did.

When we think of the senses, most of us think of the traditional five: smell, sight, hearing, taste, and touch. But some researchers believe there are actually many more than this. You may wish to consider these as well when you focus on using your senses to their full power. For example, there is a sense of balance (or equilibrioception), which helps us stay upright and stable, even if we are in motion, such as in a moving car. We have a sense of temperature (or thermoception), which allows us to sense hot and cold. A kinesthetic sense (or proprioception) allows us to keep track of our own body's position and movement. We also have pain sensors (or nociception) which allow us to feel pain. Of course, this is the body's way of telling us something is hurting. Also, there are internal senses (or interoception), which are a sense for things happening inside the body, such as hunger. Keep these senses in mind as well as the traditional five.

Benefits of the Principle

To have a brilliant mind, one must take in information. All information is received starting with the senses, and your brain's ability to interpret them. When you are learning, the more senses you use to gain information, the more channels or avenues you will have in your brain to remember and understand.

As an example of the importance of the senses in learning, consider Maria Montessori. As an educator, she noticed that children learned better when they were allowed to move, touch, and interact. In her book *The Montessori Method,* she described her daily schedule for her students as involving personal cleanliness, gymnastics, games, manual work, and caring for plants and animals. Notice that this allows more senses to get involved. Rather than just focusing on sight or hearing, her *Method* includes *all* of the traditional senses. Dr. Montessori's techniques are world-famous and have been highly useful in helping children to learn all over the world. And of course, these children grow into bright and gifted adults. Some notable alum from the Montessori schools include Jeff Bezos (Amazon founder), Jimmy Wales (Wikipedia founder), Larry Paige & Sergey Brin (Google Cofounders), and Sean "P. Diddy" Combs (hip hop recording artist).

Let's consider the benefit of our senses in another way. Think what life would be like for someone who cannot sense at all. Imagine a baby is born, and cannot see, hear, touch, smell, or taste. This would be very sad of course, but think of this as an intellectual exercise. A baby in this situation obviously could not learn anything or understand anything. This is because all information intake starts with the senses. Then the brain interprets the information. Without anything to sense, the brain has nothing to learn, understand, or interpret. The brain essentially becomes a useless organ. On the other hand, paying attention to the senses more, and perceiving more, can help lead to greater understanding. As long as you don't take in so much that you overwhelm your senses, this is a good thing.

How to Apply the Principle

Exercise weak and neglected senses

Many of us become very reliant on a few key senses. Perhaps in your profession you mostly rely on one or two senses all day. Think of which senses you use on an everyday basis. Then, think if there are any that you rarely use. Even if you do use a sense frequently, but it is always in the exact same way, you can consider that a weak sense. For example, if you work in an office you probably touch a keyboard pretty regularly. This may be stimulating when you first learn to type, but in time you become so used to the feeling that it isn't very stimulating at all. We all touch things, but do you ever touch anything new? And we all smell and taste things, but do you ever do this with new things? To keep your senses strong, they need stimulation and variety.

Now, identify your weakest sense. Take some time each day to focus on that one sense. Make it a point to use it more often, in new and interesting ways. Remember, we use nowhere near our full sensory abilities. As an example, myopia or near-sightedness is reaching epidemic proportions according to the March 2015 article "The myopia boom" by the international journal, *Nature*. Of course, genetics play some role in this. But environmental factors are also important. People are spending more and more time indoors than we used to. Donald Mutti and his colleagues at Ohio State University College of Optometry have found that children who spend more time outdoors have better vision. Some researchers believe our eyes need to see in more natural light, or at longer ranges, to develop fully. Luckily, vision is easily corrected with glasses or contact lenses, but easy solutions are not always available with our other senses. Look at these findings on vision as a lesson in the importance of keeping your senses active. Our vision goes downhill when it isn't exercised properly. Other senses likely do too.

Neglect your most dominant sense

On the other hand, you can choose to purposely neglect your most dominant sense for a short while. This will help to force you to pay more attention to other senses. For most of us, our dominant sense will be vision. As a way to neglect this sense, you can listen to a television show with your eyes closed as you imagine the scenarios in your mind. Or you can sit down on your porch outside, with your eyes closed, and pay attention to the sounds of traffic and nature. If you are feeling daring, you might even close your eyes and walk around your home, relearning the layout. You might find that even if you have lived there for years, it can still be difficult to move around efficiently. If you try this, of course, be very careful so you don't hurt yourself.

Also keep in mind that even within one type of sense, we can still neglect parts of it. For example, a sense that isn't in the traditional five would be kinesthetic sense, or motor control. In this regard, most of us are used to using one hand for most things. Since I was a child, I have enjoyed trying to use both hands for different tasks. By doing so, I felt more free and confident, knowing that I could rely on my full body, not just one side. I never thought much of this habit until at twelve years old I challenged a friend twice my size to arm wrestle. We were both right handed, so we used that hand. Of course, he beat me immediately. Embarrassed that I wasn't any challenge for him, I offered to do it again, with our left hands this time. At first he didn't want to, but eventually he agreed when I reminded him of his size compared to mine. This time, I beat him almost immediately. I exercised my full body, whereas apparently he did not.

The lesson is that it's easy to neglect a whole half of your body if you don't make a conscious effort to maintain it. This is something that takes ongoing practice, but it can be fun as long as you don't put too much pressure on yourself. You can start with brushing your teeth with your non-dominant hand. Then move on to using utensils at meals, then to writing out your name, and so forth.

By the way, my friend never agreed to arm wrestle me again. Apparently the only thing more embarrassing than losing to someone twice your size is losing to someone half your size.

Secret Principle #2: **Curiosity**

Cultivate a Deep Curiosity of the World

"There is nothing in the world that is not mysterious, but the mystery is more evident in certain things than in others: in the sea, in the eyes of the elders, in the color yellow, and in music."

— **Jorge Luis Borges**, Argentine short-story writer, essayist, poet and translator, and a key figure in Spanish-language literature.

Geniuses Who Applied the Principle

Jorge Luis Borges, Amar Bose, Albert Einstein, Michael Faraday, Stephen Hawking, Grace Hopper, Leonardo da Vinci, Norbert Wiener.

Description of the Principle

We all know what curiosity is. But a *deep curiosity* is when you want to know more. And even when you find some answers, you just have more and more questions. And so there is a deep need to know rising up from inside that can never be quenched. This is the experience many geniuses have had. In my research,

I believe it is one of the most common traits of genius, and also one of the most essential to realize your full potential.

When you are curious, this drives you to continue on a difficult problem when others have given up, and to truly understand everything about it. Curiosity is driven in part by understanding that there is a lot out there in the world that is unknown, waiting to be discovered. Then when you get out there, and you start discovering new things, often times you realize there is even more you didn't know. So you want to keep going, learning more, and the process repeats itself.

Benefits of the Principle

The late Amar Bose made breakthroughs in a variety of fields such as acoustics (e.g., the famous Bose speakers), aviation, automobiles, defense, and nuclear physics. According to an article in the December 2004 issue of *Popular Science*, titled "Better Living Through Curiosity", he claimed that the key way he was able to have such a great impact in so many fields was through his insatiable curiosity. In his daily life, he never stopped asking questions, always wondering why things did not work better, and how he could be the one to improve them.

For example, Bose's son Vanu was once with his father, who was caught driving in pouring rain with the most awful windshield wipers. "Most people would just complain about how the wipers don't work right," Vanu said, "but he was analyzing why they didn't work and thinking out loud about how to make them better. A few weeks later I saw on his desk a patent application for a new design for windshield wipers." Through asking questions and looking for better solutions for his entire life, Amar Bose created innovations and had breakthroughs in a wide range of fields. Norbert Wiener, Bose's mentor and an American mathematician, philosopher, and originator of cybernetics, has also credited his curiosity for his own accomplishments.

Curiosity is one of the best motivators to get things done. If you have curiosity, a deep desire to know and understand, then you will make much more progress than others. Many times even if they are smarter or have better preparation, the person who is more curious tends to be more driven and determined, and wins out in the end. The curious person won't get tired of working as easily. Working will feel like play, like a chance to discover something new. Many geniuses turn to science or related fields, probably because science is really about the systematic discovery of new things. It's about turning the unknown into something that is known and understood.

Another benefit of being highly curious is that you will tend to learn much more than other people. When you are deeply curious, you will be driven to learn about new things. Then, as you learn, you will come up with new questions and become curious to figure out the answers to some of these questions. There is a loop here. Curiosity leads you to learn about new things. Learning about new things makes you more curious. The opposite of this is also important to consider. If you are not curious, you do not learn about new things. If you do not learn about new things, you are not curious. A deep curiosity is a major advantage to the brilliant mind, and a lack of curiosity is a serious disadvantage.

How to Apply the Principle

Visit a museum

Sometimes we lack curiosity because we lack exposure to new things. Museums are a great place to visit for help with this. Not only are there new things to learn, but they allow us to explore what we have read about, and bring it to life. Museums can help bring out your curiosity because they turn the learning experience into something more fun and active. They often have exhibits, models, and energetic people who can explain concepts in an easy to understand way. This can help spark curiosity. Think back to the last time you visited a museum. If it has been a long while, this could be a good time to visit one. Try going to one that specializes in an interest of yours. It could be dinosaurs, science, history, art, space, marine life, or something else.

Feed your curiosity

I think many of us are naturally curious, but sometimes we don't feed it enough. Curiosity is something that must be fed to draw it out more and more. For example, when you are curious about something, it's important to investigate this further. Ask questions. Look up information. Explore. When you take that first step, you open a door that is likely to spark your curiosity further and further. Also, by being curious and learning something new, you will feel good that you are learning and understanding new things. This positive feeling will help guide you to being curious in the future and learning more again.

The problem many of us have is that we get used to having our curiosity stifled by others when we're younger, and even by ourselves as adults. Our task isn't to *become* curious, but to *reawaken* the curiosity already inside of us. Don't get in the habit of being silent when you have questions. We shouldn't think that other people will laugh at our ignorance or think less of us. By being too timid, we will actually grow more and more ignorant. And in fact, if you share your curiosity, you will often find that other people had similar questions as you, and others will be happy to inform you and share their expertise. Of course, sometimes you may receive a rude remark, but you shouldn't let those experiences ruin things for you. Be curious, and dare to ask questions. You have probably heard the saying, "There are no foolish questions, only foolish people." Consider that maybe those people are foolish because they didn't ask enough questions.

Accompany a curious friend

Do you know someone who is very curious and asks a lot of questions? An easy way to spark your curiosity is to spend more time with that person. Curiosity is not only a great way to promote learning, but it can also be entertaining to observe the mind of a super curious person. They will go to greater and greater depths, searching for new questions most people wouldn't have even considered. You may be surprised to find that curiosity can be contagious. Have you ever noticed that when an interesting question is asked, everyone all of a sudden wants to know the answer? (For example, if a baby is born exactly on the border between two countries, is it a citizen of both countries?) Unfortunately, many of us become used to getting answers with no real effort. The curious mind, however, needs to get used to working to find answers, because the true mysteries of life do not always have easy answers. The most curious people tend to be children, artists, investigators, inventors, and entrepreneurs. Seek them out, befriend them, and reawaken your curiosity with their help.

Secret Principle #3: **Adaptation**

Adapt to Changes in the Environment

"You must be shapeless, formless, like water. When you pour water in a cup, it becomes the cup. When you pour water in a bottle, it becomes the bottle. When you pour water in a teapot, it becomes the teapot. Water can drip and it can crash. Become like water, my friend."

— **Bruce Lee**, Hong Kong American martial artist, action film director, martial arts instructor, philosopher, filmmaker, and founder of Jeet Kune Do.

Geniuses Who Applied the Principle

Muhammad Ali, Marcus Aurelius, Charles Darwin, Stephen Hawking, Bruce Lee, Ernst Mach, Sun Tzu, H. G. Wells.

Description of the Principle

Adaptation is about being willing to change your approach to a scenario or problem, depending on what the situation calls for. The person who is willing to smoothly change approach depending on the situation (or new changes in a situation) is highly adaptive. The person who insists he knows the one right approach, and always takes that approach no matter the situation, is not adaptive. You can't force one solution onto every single problem you have. You have to change your approach depending on the problem.

The most certain thing we can know in life, the world, and the universe, is there will always be change. People are always growing or aging, they change their minds, and change moods. As another example of change, the Milky Way Galaxy, which we live in, is in constant motion even if we don't notice it. Actually, according to astronomers, the Milky Way is on course to collide with Andromeda (another galaxy). But don't worry, this will happen in about four billion years. Things are always changing.

The point of this book was to reveal universal principles of genius or of intelligence that could apply to most people, in many different contexts. This is perhaps the most universal principle in the book. This principle appears to apply to all kinds of life here on Earth, not just humans. The more adaptive a creature is, the more intelligent it is.

Charles Darwin said, "It is not the strongest of the species that survives, not the most intelligent that survives. It is the one that is the most adaptable to change." I believe adaptability is actually a form of intelligence. And clearly, adaptation is important to survival, but it extends beyond this to many aspects of our lives. Most of us want to do more than just survive. We want to thrive. But there are countless situations that require adaptation. In war, conditions are constantly changing, and soldiers and generals must adapt. In social situations, conversations change and people's moods can change. In a strategic competition, whether playing chess or in a wrestling match, the position of advantage can change rapidly. Knowing how to adapt is important in these systems, and in virtually *every* system.

Interestingly, people often assume that a situation will

remain static. Although many of us know things change sooner or later, in the short term we expect conditions to stay the same, or close to the same. For example, no one is probably expecting a catastrophic tornado or hurricane to hit their home tomorrow. And even less are actually prepared to deal with such an event. It is part of human nature that those who live in a good economy expect that to continue. Those who live in a good weather climate expect the same. Those who are in a positive relationship also expect this to continue. However, things can change. Entire species thrive one day and are gone the next. Those who pay the most attention to changes, even subtle ones, and how they can adjust and adapt to them, will tend to prosper the most.

Benefits of the Principle

If you make an effort to pay attention to the changes happening around you, you will be better prepared to flow with them. As Bruce Lee's quote above suggests, it is often better to flow and go along with the changes, as opposed to putting up a hard resistance to them. Even a tree abides by this principle. After there is a strong storm, with heavy gusts of wind, you don't see trees snapped in half. You see trees still standing, most of them anyway, because they bend with the pressures of the wind. They do not resist so much that they break under the pressure, like a pencil would.

Sometimes the benefit of adapting well is just to be able to survive where others have fallen. But often, surviving gives you the chance to find the best path moving forward. Those who adapt are able to survive another day, whether it is at business, war, life, or something else. Anyone who was in a situation where it was important to adapt, or risk losing big, will appreciate the benefits of being dynamic and fluid. And they will not take this principle for granted.

Let's take another perspective. Think of what happens to those who don't adapt. They lose their jobs. They lose wars. They fail, at one thing or another. Adaptors win. Those who fail to adapt to changing conditions lose. It is sad, but this is the reality.

Now, think about business owners. It is tricky to run a successful business because so many factors are changing every day. The business and its leaders need to adapt to changing consumer needs, to the competition, to new technologies, to the economy, and so forth. Those businesses which adapt the best are able to survive, and often thrive. Those who put true priority on their adaptability, by investing in research & development and starting new product lines and innovations (e.g., Amar Bose was known to do both), will have a chance at true longevity.

How to Apply the Principle

Realize almost everything is in a state of change

Adaptation is easy to understand, but not always easy to apply in real life situations. This is because adapting seems to mean very different things depending on the circumstance. But fortunately there are some common features we can focus on, which will help you to adapt in a variety of scenarios.

First, realize that everything you do is open to change. Most of us are not working within static systems, or systems that stay the same. We are working within dynamic systems, or systems that change. Static systems may exist in pure mathematics (e.g., $2 + 2$ always equals 4), but you are unlikely to find them outside of this. In the real world, many things are changing all at once and we cannot rely on an equation or calculation to give us the final answer.

Pay attention to change

Now that you know most systems tend to change, you have to pay attention to those changes, even to subtle ones. You first have to observe that something is shifting, before you can even decide what it means, and if you need to take action because of it. Of course, you won't need to adapt because of every little change you notice, but sometimes you will want to do so.

As an example of how to be adaptive, consider social situations with a group of friends. Usually, things are changing constantly, and you must adapt. One person may be upset at another. Someone else may feel insecure. Another is bragging insensitively, as others lack what he is bragging about having so much of. With constant change, it can be helpful to take an adaptive approach and to provide what the situation calls for. For example, if someone is sad, to cheer them up. If someone feels left out, to include them. And if someone says something unfriendly, to try to alleviate the matter.

If you would like another type of example, consider the sport of professional boxing. Elite fighters pay special attention to the smallest motions that indicate what the opponent plans to do next. Perhaps the eyes glance in the direction of the intended attack. Often, the shoulders sway before a punch is swung, giving a boxer enough time to dodge it. They call these telegraphed punches. Telegraphing is when you unintentionally alert your opponent as to what your plans are. To the untrained eye, the punch comes out of nowhere, landing a knockout or even fatal blow. To the trained eye, responsive to the slightest of changes, the punch is predictable and can be easily dodged.

The late Muhammad Ali was the complete master of dodging punches. In a fight with Michael Dokes in 1977, he dodged an unbelievable 21 punches within 10 seconds! Muhammad Ali always paid attention to the most subtle cues that even other professional boxers would miss. Remember his famous phrase: "Float like a butterfly, sting like a bee. His hands can't hit what his eyes can't see."

He told us himself the key to his genius technique. Always in motion, he was always adapting to the changing conditions of the fight. He was supremely well adapted to the boxing ring, or as Bruce Lee might say, shapeless and formless like water.

Condition yourself to adapt

The best way to be adaptive and to always be prepared to change is to always be in situations that require change. If you are too comfortable, too used to everything being the same, then when something changes you will be much less prepared. We have to stretch our abilities and put ourselves in new situations regularly, in order to become the most adaptive. As an example, you can travel, interact with a wide variety of people from different backgrounds, or do volunteer work in an area outside of your normal activity. To truly challenge your ability to adapt, find completely new situations to put yourself in.

According to many surveys, public speaking is often the number one fear people report having, ranking even above the fear of death. One way to become more adaptive would be to focus on overcoming fears such as this. Whether or not you have this fear, you may consider joining Toastmasters (or another public speaking group) or joining an improvisational group, where you act out different scenarios in front of an audience. It may not feel comfortable at first, but you will become more adaptive.

Secret Principle #4: **Challenge**

Pursue a High Level of Challenge

"I know that I'm not the easiest person to live with. The challenge I put on myself is so great that the person I live with feels himself challenged. I bring a lot to bear, and I don't know how not to."

— **Maya Angelou**, American poet, memoirist, and social activist.

Geniuses Who Applied the Principle

Maya Angelou, Johann Sebastian Bach, Akrit Jaswal, James Joyce, Michelangelo, Wolfgang Amadeus Mozart, Elon Musk, Isaac Newton, Marcel Proust, Sergei Rachmaninoff, Alan Turing, Leonardo da Vinci.

Description of the Principle

If you have known someone brilliant, you might have noticed that they were probably not the type of person to be easily satisfied, especially not with low quality work. Instead, they go into highly demanding fields. Or at least they will create a lot of challenges for themselves in a field, even if it isn't typically seen as highly demanding. For example, a genius may pursue medicine, art, law, engineering, physics, or something else of a high challenge. They do this because taking the easy path doesn't bring much satisfaction. Doing something easy will feel dull and pointless, whereas doing something challenging awakens the inner-genius.

Even within their own fields of expertise, which are often challenging, bright people tend to gravitate toward the tougher problems in the field. They may dream of tackling big problems, like finding the cure for cancer (e.g., as Akrit Jaswal plans to do, who conducted his first surgery at just six years old), or taking humans to Mars (e.g., as Elon Musk, founder of SpaceX, aims to do by 2024).

I believe working on tough problems can become like a drug to the genius mind. Geniuses often get used to dealing with tough problems early on. They are either quick to take them on, or sometimes other people are quick to go to them, because it is understood that this may be the only person who can solve it. The brilliant mind doesn't shy away from these difficult problems, and in time through repeated exercise of their problem-solving abilities, they become masters at solving them. Instead of a drug user needing harder *drugs*, the genius mind requires tougher and tougher *problems* to work on, to feel that they are making true progress. Through this pattern, they can reach a point where they are working on problems few other people would be able to solve.

For example, Albert Einstein's *Special Theory of Relativity*, when published, was understood by very few people. Many scientists even protested his findings, believing them to be wrong. Yet his theories have astounded us for their continuous accurate predictions. As discussed in the *National Geographic* article "Einstein May Be About to Be Proved Right – Again" this is the man who revealed light to be both a wave and a particle. He taught us that space-time can bend, which is more common around massive objects like the sun. He also showed that time is not a constant. It can slow down or speed up, depending on levels of gravity or matter. More recently, in February of 2016 Einstein made headlines when scientists at the Advanced Laser Interferometer Gravitational-Wave Observatory (LIGO) found gravitational waves (described as ripples in the fabric of space-time), which were predicted by Einstein's theories. He was such an advanced problem-solver that we are still proving him right even a hundred years after he first proposed his groundbreaking theories.

If you found Einstein's predictions hard to believe or understand, you should know that so have many other people. Yet he has been proven right time and time again. He reached this point by consistently challenging himself to solve tougher and tougher problems. But keep in mind that he was doing this from a young age. For example, even in his youth he was known for developing thought experiments in his own mind about light, time, and space. He didn't just wake up at 40 and decide to tackle the universe's biggest problems.

Benefits of the Principle

If you look to the works of great masters in history, such as the paintings of Michelangelo or Leonardo da Vinci, or the music of Rachmaninoff or Bach, or many other such masters, it is supremely clear that they rose to a great challenge. They were not interested in the easiest path. They did not back down from performing at the highest standard they possibly could. In the end, the benefit that we all enjoy is in their masterful works that have stood the test of time.

When you set a challenge for yourself that puts your abilities to the test, at first it will be extremely difficult to accomplish. You may even be unsure if you can succeed at it. But if you do press on, and through great effort complete the challenge, your abilities will grow. Soon enough, what used to be challenging will no longer seem so difficult. This is the technique many geniuses use to rise above and stand out. They pursue only the greatest of challenges. Many of them aren't interested in doing something if they are absolutely sure they can accomplish it without much effort. They want that challenge, and they accept the uncertainty of whether they can accomplish it, because they know this is how intellectual growth happens.

How to Apply the Principle

Focus on your ideal level of challenge

The exact challenges you face will of course vary depending on what field you choose to work in. But either way you will want to pursue the ideal level of challenge for yourself. This can take some practice to figure out. It will depend on your current abilities, and on how much energy you have to work on difficult problems or in difficult situations.

To find your ideal level of challenge, first you should start with a challenging task, but not necessarily a larger goal that may take months to accomplish. The best situation is if you can choose a task that will take you a day or less to complete. You want a high level of challenge, but not so high that it becomes impossible or completely unrealistic to do. The right challenge will be different for everyone. If you are a beginner, you have to be careful not to choose something too difficult. And if you are highly advanced, you have to be careful not to choose something too easy.

One way to help get to an ideal level of challenge is to alter the time limits that you allow yourself to do a given task. If a task normally takes you eight hours to complete, you can attempt to do it in six, for example. You may look for ways to speed up your progress, avoid wasting time, or look for unnecessary steps that can be eliminated.

Stretch your abilities

Another way of challenging yourself is to offer to work on tasks that are above your current level. Don't stretch so far above your level that you have no understanding of what you need to do, however. Look for opportunities where you understand the idea of what needs to be done, but you don't necessarily know *all* of the details involved. It helps if you can find someone at a higher level that you can assist. That way, you can learn and challenge yourself while not feeling too pressured if you are unable to complete the task on your own. Remember, the point is to challenge yourself, so avoid asking questions on every minor detail. Make an effort to find solutions for yourself.

Secret Principle #5: **Vision**

Turn Your Vision into a Reality

"All of our dreams can come true, if we have the courage to pursue them."

— **Walt Disney,** American entrepreneur, animator, voice actor, and film producer.

Geniuses Who Applied the Principle

Walt Disney, Henry Ford, Bill Gates, Steve Jobs, Vladimir Nabokov.

Description of the Principle

When you have a vision, you will see in your mind's eye a completed magnificent project, perhaps all in a flash. But it will be so vivid that it will be as real as day. Imagine holding the *Mona Lisa* in your mind *before it was actually created*, every last detail. It exists in your mind, and you feel that you must share it with the world. Or imagine holding Disney World in your mind, seeing the children happily playing among the rides with Disney characters all around. You see it so clearly, the joy and laughter of families visiting from around the world, that it seems ridiculous to not create it, no matter what it costs you. Other people may not understand. They may even think you are foolish when you decide to create something on such a grand scale. But in your mind, it will already be complete. It is just a matter of executing the process to turn the vision into a reality. It seems foolish not to create your vision. This is what it means to have a vision for the genius mind.

Geniuses often have a very specific vision of what they wish to accomplish. They know what they want, and they aren't willing to compromise on it. Brilliant people tend to look for the best people who can help turn their vision into a reality. They may listen to criticisms, but in the end will have justifications and insist on doing things the way they imagined them. You have to understand that by the time a brilliant person has a vision, usually he is at the peak of his field. Anyone offering advice isn't likely to have as much experience. In the end, the people who disagree or don't understand the vision will either need to come to agree and understand, or leave the project altogether.

The origins of a vision are hard to pin down, even for the brilliant minds that have them. It may actually be the result of a great deal of experience in a field, a deep intuition, and partly it may be something the genius wants to see brought to reality for their own personal fulfilment. This principle can be difficult to grasp if you have not experienced it yourself. But this is something that has been a reoccurring theme for many of the world's brightest minds.

Benefits of the Principle

Steve Jobs, the founder and former CEO of Apple, had the vision for a series of products he believed would change the way people received their information and sought out entertainment. He had a strong vision of his product ideas and their place in the future. Because of this, he wasn't concerned with what specific people said they wanted Apple to design. Jobs told *Businessweek:* "A lot of times, people don't know what they want until you show it to them." And he proceeded to show it to them. First, he released the Apple Computer. Then he had the vision to see that people wanted to carry much more than a CD's worth of music with them, and they wanted it to be portable, so he released the iPod. After that, he foresaw that the iPod would eventually become irrelevant as phones would soon have the ability to carry music, and people would want to do everything on a single device. That is when he started working on the iPhone. His visions were right time and time again. When a vision is accurate, and based on experience and deep understanding, the benefits can be immense.

Turning a vision into a reality, or attempting to do so, can be the biggest project of one's life. It will require money, time, resources, expertise, assistants, and so forth. This can be a massive challenge, but the benefit is that it can also be the biggest learning experience of a lifetime. It is important to see this through to the end to be absolutely certain if the vision will work out as expected. Another obvious benefit of a vision is that if you manage to execute it and be successful with it, you will end up with a fantastic work of genius that countless people can enjoy or use in some way.

How to Apply the Principle

Focus on gaining mastery

The best way to apply this principle is not to make an attempt to have a vision. By their nature, they will happen when you have gained sufficient mastery, when you understand what you are doing so well that there are few people more knowledgeable than you in your specific area. You will likely feel that you know what you are doing so well that what you do, whether it is play piano, scientific research, or design buildings, is actually an extension of yourself. You no longer clearly separate what you do from yourself. When you reach that level, you will begin to know things intuitively. You won't need to calculate and think deeply about every single problem that arises. You will have so much experience that your intuitive grasp will allow you to understand situations rapidly, based on seeing so many patterns over many years. At that point it is more likely that you will experience a powerful vision.

Consider the risks involved

This principle will be one of the most challenging ones to apply. Although it has been used successfully by many brilliant minds, you should take some caution with the principle. Given that visions tend to be in depth and require large amounts of time and money, it is important to consider the possible downsides. You should at least think them through and decide if it is a risk worth taking. This is a principle where we may hear about people like Steve Jobs and Walt Disney, but it is likely there are others who pursued their vision at all costs, and ultimately did not succeed in their efforts, and so we have never heard about them. Keep this in mind and weigh the pros and cons of pursuing your vision. Ask yourself if the time is right.

Secret Principle #6: **Uniqueness**

Embrace Your Uniqueness

"If a man does not keep pace with his companions, perhaps it is because he hears a different drummer. Let him step to the music which he hears, however measured or far away."

— **Henry David Thoreau,** American author, poet, philosopher, abolitionist, naturalist, tax resister, development critic, historian, and a leading transcendentalist.

Geniuses Who Applied the Principle

Thomas Edison, Albert Einstein, F. Buckminster Fuller, Andy Kaufman, Jackson Pollock, Henry David Thoreau, Leonardo da Vinci.

Description of the Principle

Great minds in history tend to not place too much importance on following conventions. Whether they are social or workplace conventions, the genius is much more likely to approach problems in his own way. They either lack fear of being seen as different, they push through the fear, or they may even find pleasure in being seen as different. Often, from a young age they tend to think in unique ways, and approach problems and situations in a different way than others would. But they also come to realize that just because they do not do things in the same way as others, doesn't make them wrong.

Geniuses may appear unconventional, possibly even eccentric or quirky. Sometimes, though, a bright mind is able to see much more of a problem, or further into the implications of a problem, than other people. A brilliant mind may choose a path no one else even realized existed. This is a part of what it means to be a genius, to see options that other people may not even have considered as being an actual option.

A reason for such uniqueness can be that the genius has something on the mind of such a high priority, that all other things no longer matter. Being fashionable, socially graceful, or even eating and sleeping on a normal schedule, may all seem unimportant when someone is working on big problems and feels they must be solved.

For instance, according to *Time* Magazine, Buckminster Fuller, an unconventional thinker and inventor, experimented with polyphasic sleep – or sleeping throughout the day, taking 30 minute naps every six hours instead of sleeping all at once at night. Although he probably didn't care what people thought about it, he eventually stopped because it conflicted too much with the schedules of his business associates.

Another strange example, according to 20th century history expert Jennifer Rosenberg at About.com, is that Albert Einstein did not wear socks. It seems he found them unnecessary and uncomfortable. Or, you might remember him more for his unruly and wild hair. However, keep in mind that brilliant people don't usually make it a goal in itself to be unique. Instead, they have other more important goals, and in order for them to make the most progress, they end up doing things that are much different from the norm.

Benefits of the Principle

Thinking unconventionally can be helpful because it allows us to be less limited. When you open up your thinking to ways that seem forbidden or closed off, you give yourself more options as to how to handle problems and find solutions. Thinking in such ways can spark creativity and help with making breakthroughs.

You may have noticed that instead of doing things in a new, interesting, or unique way, people often do their tasks in the same way, again and again. Often enough, they are instructed to do things this way by their teachers or bosses, for the sake of efficiency. However, it can be a competitive advantage to find unique ways to do tasks that still provide a good solution. It is always possible that a different way of doing something is actually a massive improvement over the usual way that it is done. This is essentially what it means to be creative. People who are more open to approaching problems in new ways are often the ones who are more likely to make a great discovery. They do not concern themselves with the many limits most of us are automatically restrained by. And this helps them to see more options, and to dare to be different, and ultimately to make a brilliant breakthrough.

As an example of the benefits of being unique, consider Jackson Pollock, the abstract expressionist painter, famous for his drip-style painting technique. Historians have also called this style "action painting", because the paintings are created by making brush strokes in the air, while the canvas lies on the floor. According to the Khan Academy course offered by the Museum of Modern Art (MoMA), "The Paintings of Jackson Pollock", this occurs through quick and fluid dance-like motions. They are not created through brush strokes made on an upright canvas, which is the way most paintings are made.

Pollock created art in a way other artists had never even considered. He not only created new paintings, but he also created his own artistic form, rather than sticking to conventions. Part of his ingeniousness was that his paintings were unexpected and counter to what we would normally view as art. But he perfected this original technique and created masterful artwork with it.

How to Apply the Principle

Find people who will embrace your uniqueness

Fear is something that can limit your ability to think in unconventional ways. Fear of saying something unacceptable, something that doesn't sound intelligent, or something that is rejected as being ridiculous. A way to help alleviate this fear of thinking differently, or being different, is to seek out a group that is very open to new ideas and different ways of thinking, a group that actually encourages this. That way, it will feel more natural and safe to come up with your own unique ideas. You will not have to fear the responses of anyone. For example, considering how much time we spend at work, you may want to pursue a work environment that is open to new ideas, new ways of thinking, and doesn't look at these things as a problem or something to be avoided.

Practice thinking in unique ways

To think more uniquely, you can practice building up unconventional thoughts. For example, think of two random words, such as 'rock' and 'plant'. Don't worry if they are related or not, just think of two different things as fast as you can. Then try to think up how the two objects or concepts may be related. Encourage yourself to think outside of your normal ways of thinking. Your responses do not need to be completely logical. If you would like, you can take a moment to think up a few examples of how 'rock' and 'plant' are related, and then see how they compared to mine in the following paragraph.

Did you come up with some ideas? Here is what I came up with. As an example response for 'rock' and 'plant', both are things that don't move on their own. Also, both are things that can be used for decoration. As an outside the box example, Robert *Plant* was the lead guitarist for the musical group Led Zeppelin, who played a type of *rock* music. This is a more interesting response, because both the use of the word 'plant' and 'rock' are not the ones that usually first come to mind. You can also turn this into a game or contest with friends if you wish, to see who can come up with more unique and interesting responses.

Secret Principle #7: **Perfection**

Operate at the Highest Standards; Strive for Perfection

"If you're going to try, go all the way. Otherwise, don't even start. This could mean losing girlfriends, wives, relatives and maybe even your mind. It could mean not eating for three or four days. It could mean freezing on a park bench. It could mean jail. It could mean derision. It could mean mockery – isolation. Isolation is the gift. All the others are a test of your endurance, of how much you really want to do it. And you'll do it, despite rejection and the worst odds. And it will be better than anything else you can imagine. If you're going to try, go all the way. There is no other feeling like that. You will be alone with the gods, and the nights will flame with fire. You will ride life straight to perfect laughter. It's the only good fight there is."

— **Charles Bukowski**, German-American poet, novelist, and short story writer.

Geniuses Who Applied the Principle

Charles Bukowski, James Joyce, Prince Rogers Nelson (the late singer-songwriter, more commonly known as just Prince),

Marcel Proust, Nikola Tesla, Leo Tolstoy, Leonardo da Vinci.

Description of the Principle

A common theme among geniuses is that they place high demands on themselves. They aspire to do the best work they absolutely can, and they consider it unacceptable to fall short of this. The brilliant mind is usually focused on something he views as extremely important. Because of this, he tends to be much more driven than most people to meet the highest standards possible. The genius will do anything to set up the best possible conditions to produce the best work. This could mean finding just the right materials for a piece of artwork. It could mean taking extra time when writing a novel or nonfiction book, getting inside the characters heads, or traveling to real life places that the book is based off of. It means doing whatever it takes to create a masterpiece.

This principle drives home the point that to produce a genius level work is not something that happens with little care, effort, or investment of time and money. It doesn't happen by accident. The genius is often one who commits to the highest standards, and does this not just occasionally. It won't happen just on one project because the boss said it was important. Instead, this is a personal quality that the brilliant mind will always carry.

A mistake people often make is to think that they are in a part of life where what they are doing does not matter much. They think they have little impact with their work, and do not expect much from themselves. This is not the mindset that the brightest minds will have. No matter the situation, they will tend to look for ways to be the best. When you have this approach of doing the best work that you can, even when the task seems trivial, you will soon be given tougher tasks, greater responsibility, and bigger rewards. And even if you aren't, your mind will be working at a higher level. You may notice details that can be improved. Maybe one day you will have the opportunity to set up your own business that competes with the one you are working for now. If you have truly done your best, and tried to always improve at your work, when you have the opportunity to rise to a higher level, you will be prepared for it.

Benefits of the Principle

Let's discuss Nikola Tesla, the Serbian American inventor and engineer best known for his work on the design of the modern alternating current (AC) electricity supply system. In his autobiography titled *My Inventions*, he mentioned how he once started reading a book written by Voltaire. Whenever he started something, he felt that he must finish it. To his dismay, he realized that Voltaire had written 100 full volumes. Tesla felt that since he had started reading one volume, that he must finish all of them. This is how perfectionistic he was. He did end up reading them all, but it was unpleasant for him because he knew it was a distraction from his work. He felt such a strong need to complete the things he started, that he didn't feel he had any other option than to finish the 100 volumes.

You might think that actually, this section is supposed to be about the *benefits* of the principle. Interestingly, it seems like a negative that he was so perfectionistic he could barely control it. On the other hand, Tesla had so many brilliant breakthroughs and discoveries that surely his thoroughness and perfectionism in his work helped him in life. For example, according to a report titled "Nikola Tesla's Patents" by Snežana Šarbohhe, he reportedly held 116 original patents in 26 countries. If his standards had been lower, he probably wouldn't have been the brilliant genius we know him to be.

When you place high standards on your work, you are much more likely to produce top quality work. Half of the battle to greatness is just to pursue it, to commit to it. Those who do not even attempt it will never get there. After you commit to top level work, you are much more likely to build upon your skills. By pushing and challenging yourself, you will be learning new things, expanding your abilities into new areas. Many people show up to work, but geniuses truly put in the work (Principle #9), and in doing so they help themselves to reach a higher level of knowledge, understanding, and performance.

It is important for you to understand another key benefit of this principle, that greatness attracts greatness. When you commit to working at the highest standards, and refuse to lower them, you will begin to attract other brilliant minds. They may become interested in helping you or collaborating with you in some way, helping your skills reach an even higher level. You will find that brilliant minds are the best to challenge you, and to push you to do even better work. There is always the chance that you meet strong resistance, if they prefer to approach the work in a different way than you. But keep an open mind. There is always something you can learn from other brilliant people.

In a lesson on how greatness can attract greatness, consider the late musical artist, Prince. In the *Hollywood Reporter* article "Prince's Performance Perfectionism", Patrick Whalen, Prince's former production manager made some comments about Prince. He said, "He always demanded the best," and, "He never settled." Whalen also mentioned that when he first began working for Prince, he was asked to create a specific lighting effect for one of his shows. Whalen immediately told Prince this wasn't possible. Prince looked him in the eyes intensely, and Whalen couldn't believe what he said: "So what you're telling me is that in the one second it took you to say 'no', you left your body and exhausted every possibility?" Whalen stammered back, "I'll get back to you." He never made the mistake of saying "No" to Prince again, and because of it, he expected more from himself and grew in his own abilities too. The lesson here is that the great ones who demand only the best will attract a similar energy, helping to elevate themselves and those around them to an even higher status.

How to Apply the Principle

Expect more from yourself

A simple way to apply this principle is to practice expecting more from yourself. Think about the bar you normally set for yourself in your work and in your life. Set it higher. If you feel more comfortable, you can raise the bar a little bit, then raise it again, and repeat this over and over. In time, you will eventually be pursuing an extremely high standard. Expect better performance from yourself, and you can achieve it.

Review your work

Also, when you do finish a job, don't be so quick to mark it as final. Do a last review of your work to see if there are any corrections you could make. Much of the time, we are in a hurry to get things done so we can move on to the next task. Sometimes you have to stop and think that if the task you are doing is important, then it needs to be done right. You need to check the work. And if it isn't important, why are you doing it in the first place? It is either important enough to do it right, and check the work, or it isn't important enough to be done at all.

Always do your best

Whatever work you are doing, even if it is not something you are especially interested in, you should take it as an opportunity to practice doing your best work. It is easy to do your best when you are working on something you love, such as a hobby. But the true test is to do your best when you would rather be doing something else. Keep in mind that the tasks you work on are probably important for someone. This could be your boss, a client, or for yourself. You should aim to do work you enjoy and are interested in, but if occasionally you find yourself doing something you would rather not do, practice doing your best work anyway. Of course, if you repeatedly find yourself in situations doing work and tasks you don't want to do, it may be time to make a change.

Secret Principle #8: **Perseverance**

Persevere in the Face of Obstacles; Don't Give Up

"It is no good getting furious if you get stuck. What I do is keep thinking about the problem but work on something else. Sometimes it is years before I see the way forward. In the case of information loss and black holes, it was 29 years."

— **Stephen Hawking,** English theoretical physicist, cosmologist, author and Director of Research at the Centre for Theoretical Cosmology within the University of Cambridge.

Geniuses Who Applied the Principle

Jane Austen, Ludwig van Beethoven, Miguel de Cervantes, Marie Curie, Fyodor Dostoyevski, Albert Einstein, Temple Grandin, Stephen Hawking, Helen Keller, Isaac Newton, Marcel Proust, Ben Underwood.

Description of the Principle

It is one thing to challenge yourself, or to pursue a high standard, but it's another when you are dealt with obstacle after obstacle, and kicked down no matter what you try. Eventually, this can become tiring and demotivating. After too many troubles, it is likely that anyone would want to give up and quit. The difference is that the genius mind will often refuse to quit, no matter what kinds of obstacles there are.

For example, at 21, Stephen Hawking was diagnosed with amyotrophic lateral sclerosis (ALS), also known as motor neurone disease or Lou Gehrig's disease. It would gradually destroy his muscles, paralyze him, and it was expected to kill him within two to three years. Somehow, defying all of the odds, he is still alive at the time of this writing (2016), at the age of 74. I believe part of the reason he is still alive is because he was unwilling to allow the disease to take over him without fighting it. He was unwilling to give up. He always continued to work as a theoretical physicist, even when he could no longer speak or control his movements. He has also been greatly helped by technology, which allows him to communicate. If you have heard him speak, his voice now sounds electronic, because it is with the aid of a computer.

Consider this example of his perseverance. A few years after his diagnosis, his muscles were clearly weakening. It had become a huge feat for him to even walk. He had a flight of stairs in his home, and even as his muscles were atrophying, he would climb them. He refused help from others in this. It took all of his energy and willpower, but he did it. It is very fitting that one of the brightest minds of our times would have that much will to persevere despite the obstacles. Clearly, he has taken a similar approach in his scientific life as well (e.g., see quote above). No matter what obstacles came his way, whether intellectual or physical, he always fought through them, and didn't allow them to defeat him.

When life hands us challenges that seem too tough, it can be instinctive to back up and look for an easier way. On the other hand, the genius does everything in their power to persist, to fight, and to make progress even in the face of major obstacles. It is a misconception that everything comes easily to the genius. The greatest geniuses of all history are often people who persisted through many obstacles, and in that process came to a deep understanding that surpassed their peers. Remember that if a brilliant person appears to understand everything easily, it is most likely through much preparation, largely through persevering even when the obstacles seemed too big to overcome.

Benefits of the Principle

When Bobby Fischer (former World Chess Champion) studied chess, he came to realize that many of the greatest chess books were written in Russian. You should know that the Russian players were known to completely dominate chess at the highest levels. To give you an idea of their level of domination, they had schools for children dedicated solely to learning chess. And top players were funded by government programs so they could dedicate their lives to it without distraction. The USA had nothing like this. Chess in the USA was a hobby. In Russia, it was their national pride and a way of life.

The problem was that Bobby Fischer was *not* from Russia. He was from the United States, and he did not know Russian. While most Americans had no access to the treasure trove of information in these Russian chess books, Fischer decided he needed to learn what was inside of them. He wanted to be the best chess player in the world, and to do so he understood that he needed to learn from the best resources. And they were written in Russian. Fischer decided to study the language seriously. He was so committed to chess that he was willing to struggle through learning a new, unfamiliar language, just to improve his game. He studied the challenging foreign language, whereas most other top level chess players never even considered it.

Ultimately, it paid off for Fischer. He became the best player in the world, defeating Boris Spassky to win the World Chess Championship in 1972. He proved that he could beat the Russians at their own game, and no other American came even close to his ability. Sooner or later, his kind of perseverance pays off. I should note that Bobby Fischer stopped playing the game professionally after he won, and therefore he lost the title quickly. His accomplishments were highly impressive nonetheless. Many people believe he was the greatest chess player who ever lived.

Persisting and moving forward even when there are difficult obstacles, like Bobby Fischer did, is obviously not easy. This is why most people look for the alternative path. They search for an easier road. And that is fine, but it is not the path to genius. When we commit to doing something, no matter the challenges that come our way, we become much stronger in our intellect, our understanding, and our abilities. We move forward on the path to genius. Keep in mind that the brightest people will often seek the most difficult challenges. They are not worried about obstacles. In fact, they look forward to them. Brilliant minds understand that the benefits of obstacles and hardships are too great to ignore. The genius will be uninterested in a path without obstacles. The easy way is not what they are after. They are after the advancement of the mind and true understanding.

Where many people are shortsighted is that they will see an obstacle that seems impossible, and its difficulty becomes all that they can focus on. They build it up in their minds to be even bigger, more worrisome, and fearsome than it truly is. By focusing too much on the problem, it becomes bigger and bigger. The brilliant mind, however, recognizes that it is possible to overcome the obstacle. They become determined to show that it can be done. They focus on the possible ways to solve the problem, not on how impossible it seems to deal with. When you persist through obstacles, and do so repeatedly, you will begin to acquire an aura of genius. Things that appeared impossible to others will be completely within your grasp. Your reward will be that things which once cost you much strain, will now appear to come from you as if without effort.

How to Apply the Principle

Reframe obstacles as opportunities

Again, here we have a principle that seems easy to apply, but can be difficult to do so successfully. This is because most of us don't want to deal with challenge. It is a natural part of human nature to want to do things we are already good at. This is where we feel comfortable. On the other hand, it is uncomfortable to try to overcome an obstacle. Here is an idea to help you tackle obstacles more comfortably. We have to retrain ourselves to see obstacles in a new way, so we can make true progress on them rather than feel overwhelmed. When you see an obstacle, forget that it is a problem, and something that needs to be overcome. Instead, look at this as an opportunity. Don't think about how tough it is, how impossible it is, and how ridiculous it is to even try it. Instead, think about the rare opportunity you have to truly challenge yourself, learn, and grow. Think opportunity, not obstacle.

Create your own obstacles

The best way to prepare ourselves for obstacles is to get used to overcoming them regularly. If you get used to solving tough problems, dealing with tough situations, and getting through them, then you will be much better prepared to deal with obstacles that are truly big. Others will have no idea how to handle them, because they aren't used to it, and they are likely to be frightened or too stressed to take the best course of action. The geniuses are the ones that handle obstacles that are so large hardly anyone else, even experts, can fathom dealing with them. Even if there are no obstacles in your life, create them. Make tasks harder than they are supposed to be, in order to be prepared when a true problem presents itself. Consider this training, so you are always ready for the next big problem.

Put in the Work

"Opportunity is missed by most people because it is dressed in overalls and looks like work."

— **Thomas Edison,** American inventor and businessman, owner of 2,332 patents.

Geniuses Who Applied the Principle

Thomas Edison, Albert Einstein, Bobby Fischer, William Shakespeare, Nikola Tesla, Leonardo da Vinci.

Description of the Principle

This principle may seem obvious, but there is a persistent obsession with the genius mind, as if this were all it took to be truly brilliant. The mind, of course, is important, but do not make the mistake of overlooking this principle. There have been many talented people who were never motivated enough, or could never be bothered to put in the work necessary to make all of their brilliant ideas or abilities come to life. Those are the ones who are not recognized as great geniuses in history. Perhaps you know someone who appears to be quite brilliant, someone who always has ideas for how to fix things, for inventions, and ideas on what needs to be done to fix world issues. But it's a much different thing to *talk* things through, as opposed to *work* things through. Some brilliant people prefer to think or talk things through first, then go to work. Others go to work first, look at the results, think and talk it through, and make improvements as they can. Either way can work. But going to work is a key step.

Going to work isn't something only associated with geniuses. Obviously, most people need to work to earn a living. But if you study the most brilliant minds, you will find that they are often the most eager to work and to make progress in their field. They do not shy away from doing hard work at all. Often, they are willing to go above and beyond what most people would consider doing. Whereas many of us show up to work, and go through the motions that are requested of us, the genius truly puts in the work. They invest great amounts of time in their understanding of the field. They do not expect others to show them how to do everything. They don't just show up to work. They break new ground and make new discoveries, which requires a much more advanced level of work than most people are willing to commit to.

Nikola Tesla reported in his biography, *My Inventions*, that he worked every day from 10:30 a.m. to 5:00 a.m. He was clearly willing to put in the work, as this is eighteen and a half hours per day. He also worked so hard that when he was at university, the professors wrote letters to his father that Tesla was working so much that they were worried he could die from it. Of course, Tesla pushed the limits, and it isn't advised to work so hard that we harm our health. But if you look into the lives of many prominent people, geniuses, leaders, and other successful people, you will find that they are typically closer in work schedule to Tesla than they are to someone who works the bare minimum, concerned more with their next break period than they are with doing good work. To make great progress at anything will require putting in the work. It isn't sufficient just to have the genius mindset alone.

Benefits of the Principle

The benefits of this principle should be clear. The *work* is where things actually get done. Without work, none of the creations we admire would exist. Michelangelo was an artistic genius before he painted the Sistine Chapel. Nonetheless, what makes Michelangelo who he is, and other geniuses who they are, is that they weren't content just to have the brilliant mind. They got to their mythical status not just through ingenious thoughts, but through putting in the work, time and again. By the time they were true masters of the craft, the work they put out was extraordinary, and to us may seem impossible, as if no mortal human could have created such masterpieces. But the truth is that continuously putting in the work required, and learning from it, will take you a long way.

Get used to working the earliest in your life that you can. It is a frequent mistake to think that you will do the work later. Those who make real progress commit to doing it now. This habit is an important one, perhaps the most important one of all. As a warning on neglecting putting in the work, you should know that there are plenty of bright young minds, who learn new things easily, without even trying. It is effortless, and requires no work. Later on, as these children advance into more challenging subjects, it comes as a surprise that they may have to work to understand something. By that point, some of these children are set up for failure because they don't even understand the concept of work. It doesn't feel right to them, because they have gotten so used to having it easy. One of the most destructive beliefs to genius is that you can make a big breakthrough without putting in the work. Be sure to ban such thoughts from your mind.

A final benefit of this principle is that since many people are reluctant to do truly hard work, this is a way that you can stand out from others. The amount of time you work, how focused you are, and how much you value the work, are all things you can choose to make progress on. If you place more priority on your work, you will find yourself gradually moving up the ranks, gaining recognition and reputation as someone who does a great job. Eventually, this may evolve into brilliant or genius level creations.

How to Apply the Principle

Commit to the work

The simplest change to make is to commit to working more. By spending more time at your work, you can improve your skills, and make more progress in your goals. You don't necessarily need to work like Tesla, or work 80 hours per week, but it is important to realize that to make great progress will require true commitment. If you dedicate yourself to a project only when you have 'extra free time', it is unlikely to ever get done. Set a schedule, make goals, and stick to it.

Another thing you can do is to actually think through your work patterns. Aim not just to work more, but to accomplish more for the time you put in. Identify the most critical parts of your job, and be sure to always keep those in mind. Consider asking your boss to clarify what they value the most. As an example, if you work with a variety of clients, the boss might want you to pay special attention to long-time customers. Perhaps those return customers are responsible for most of the purchases in your business. It is important to keep your eyes open and make sure you have the biggest effect that you can in your work. Do not allow yourself to become distracted. For instance, avoid working on so many projects at once that you are unable to do the best job at any of them.

Know your motivations

Another important consideration is your motivation. Those geniuses who have worked the hardest have often been the most motivated. It can be a good idea to ask yourself what your motivations are. Are they in the right place, or do you work simply as a job, to earn income? For the most brilliant geniuses, their work is more than just a job. It rises to a level of being a part of who they are personally. You can fight against motivation, but true genius creations can require decades of persistence. Without motivation, it is very difficult to create the best work. To truly meet your genius potential will require a *deep motivation*, and a willingness to put in the work. This combination is not easy to find, but it can truly open up the path to genius for you.

Remove obstacles that prevent your best performance

Focus on anything you can do to make improvements and increase your work output. Sometimes we need assistance. Are you trying to work on too many things at once? Perhaps it is time to find a helper to move things along more smoothly. Ask where your abilities would make the most impact. If you are wasting time on tasks anyone could do, delegate those tasks to a subordinate, so you can focus on the more challenging problems you need to work on. The key is, whatever the greatest obstacle is to your advancement at work, focus on overcoming it. It may be that you need more funding, more resources, assistance, or something else. Identify what is holding you back from doing your best work, and tackle this first so you can make a breakthrough in your progress.

Learning

"I have never met a man so ignorant that I couldn't learn something from him."

— **Galileo Galilei,** Italian astronomer, physicist, engineer, philosopher, and mathematician who played a major role in the scientific revolution during the Renaissance.

There is no debate that having the will and desire to learn is one of the most important aspects of genius. In order to improve your mind, think more like a genius, and act more like one, you must commit to learning and growing intellectually. Without this desire and commitment, the path to genius will be sealed off.

Brilliant minds not only make a habit of learning, but learning is a joyful thing to look forward to, and a way of life. Many of them don't even consciously think about what they are going to learn on any given day. Instead, their curiosity feeds into their desire to learn. They surround themselves with tools and resources for constant learning, such as great books. They have friends and colleagues who have made learning into a way of life, and so it only seems completely natural to always be learning.

This section is about how geniuses pursue learning. We are probably all aware that learning is important for bright minds. Knowledge doesn't come out of thin air, it must be acquired somehow. We will explore the secret principles geniuses have used throughout history to excel at learning. You will then be able to apply them for yourself, and pursue your path to genius.

Secret Principle #10: **Initiative**

Take Initiative in Learning New Things

"Children are sitting there and they are taught and told what to believe. They are passive from the very beginning, and one must be very aggressive intellectually to have a high IQ."

— **Marilyn vos Savant,** Magazine columnist, author, lecturer, and playwright, known for having the highest recorded IQ according to the Guinness Book of Records, a category the publication has since retired.

Geniuses Who Applied the Principle

Thomas Edison, Michael Faraday, Johann Wolfgang von Goethe, Marilyn vos Savant, Henry David Thoreau.

Description of the Principle

Most of us realize learning is important. We go to school, and we have teachers that can help us with this. However, we often get too used to being instructed on what we need to do, and how we need to do it. This is the way many of us learn, but eventually everyone reaches a point where they need to learn for themselves. Perhaps your teacher is busy, or wasn't able to explain a concept well enough, or you have advanced enough that you no longer have a formal teacher or instructor. Perhaps you *are* the instructor now. But in many fields, continuous learning is important to making real progress. There is a constant stream of new and changing information to make sense of. For example, the internet has so much new information every day that it would be impossible to keep up with all of it. In any case, we need to know how to learn regularly, with or without the aid of others, to stay up to date on the latest information.

Realize that not all brilliant minds were blessed with wonderful teachers from a young age. Michael Faraday (a scientist known for his work in electromagnetism), for example, was not born into a family with the best connections to help him become a great scientist. He took the initiative, in reading scientific books, taking detailed notes of professor's lectures, and being persistent in trying to work with a major chemist of the time, Humphry Davy. Isaac Newton was not born into a family of scientists or teachers either. Newton was the son of a farmer, and his parents could offer him no assistance in the world of science. But he learned and excelled at it, despite his upbringing. He didn't make an excuse that there was no one to instruct him. In fact, both of these scientists took the initiative.

This principle is meant to serve as a key reminder that it is not others who control our fate. In fact, we hold more cards than we think we do, in the direction our lives will take. The power of knowledge and learning is so great that it can change our lives and open new doors. Just think, if brilliant minds in more difficult times were able to find a way to learn, then surely we can too. We live in the Information Age, where the internet provides us access to virtually limitless information. There is no excuse whatsoever to be ignorant in the topics we would like to master. If anything, the problem of today's learners is the opposite of the problem centuries ago. We may suffer from too much information, which can become paralyzing. The key is to prioritize, and to focus on small steps, and not try to learn everything all at once.

Benefits of the Principle

When you take command of your own learning, you will no longer be completely dependent on any one curriculum, or on what anyone else decides you should learn. You will be able to learn beyond the limits imposed by your educational system. For example, as a biology student, you may choose to study aquatic life, or desert life forms, even if those topics are neglected in your formal studies. You may even choose to learn the history of life, going back to the earliest lifeforms. And of course, you can even delve into other topic areas, such as the physics of life, or you could study how we can improve the conditions of the Earth to be the best for all life. When you choose what you want to learn, you will make much more progress in your areas of interest, and you will learn how to learn.

Of course, you don't have to make the choice of having a teacher *or* guiding your own learning. The best option is probably to do both. This may provide the greatest benefit. It is important to have some structure when you are learning, especially when starting out, because you don't know enough yet to understand what the most important things to learn are. But it is also good to be free to explore what you are most interested and curious about. Otherwise, the learning experience will become stale, and you may grow bored with it and stop learning altogether.

This is a principle where the benefits are clearer if we look at those who do not abide by it. If we get too comfortable in following a set curriculum, we lose our sense of control. And through this feeling, the learning will not feel especially important. We will begin to learn in order to meet the criteria, such as to get praise, a grade, or a job. The last reason on the mind will be that we are learning to learn, to understand, to gain mastery. Being active in your learning pursuits will help avoid this problem. You will have chosen that you want to learn something, and you will know exactly why. And any formal teachers and classes will be viewed as just an aid in the process, not just a chore to get through.

How to Apply the Principle

Seek answers to your own questions

Practice coming up with your own questions, and then seek your own answers to them. You can look through any sources you wish. There are libraries, online sources, and experts you can ask. But it can be powerful to take the initiative and to choose your own direction. Then, the sources you use will just be tools on your journey to greater learning. Rather than blindly following a set path, you will be creating your own.

Look up information

When you come across something you do not understand, perhaps a word or concept, look it up yourself. Marilyn vos Savant (from quote above), known for her high IQ, has stated in a 1986 interview given by Harold Channer that when she asked questions as a child, her parents told her to look things up for herself. It is good to ask questions, but if there is not an expert right at your side, your best source of information will probably be through your own research. Understand that if you do not put any work into getting an answer, you will probably just as easily forget the information. Also, a dictionary, or other authoritative sources, can give you more accurate information and detail than most people can give you. Many experts will simply recall what they have read, and this is information you may already have access to online, in books, dictionaries, or other sources.

Take advantage of free resources

If you have access to the internet, or even a good library, there is no excuse for remaining ignorant. I believe this is an especially important point to make for those who may not have access to the best formal education, or may not have the income or time to commit to it. Realize that there are a variety of high quality free resources online to learn virtually anything. You can start with a simple Google search, or you can read a free report I wrote, about the best free learning resources.

Here is a link to the signup page to get the report: mentalmax. net/EN. Type it into your web browser (I just ask for your email address so I can send you updates on my new books).

Secret Principle #11: **Foundations**

Build a Solid Foundation of Knowledge

"If you go and talk to most people, they mean well but they don't have much of a breadth on education, of knowledge of understanding what the real issues are and therefore they listen to pundits on television who tell them what they are supposed to think and they keep repeating that until pretty soon they say, 'Oh, well that must be true.'"

— **Ben Carson,** retired American neurosurgeon, known for successfully separating conjoined twins, and former candidate for President of the United States.

Geniuses Who Applied the Principle

Aristotle, Jorge Luis Borges, Ben Carson, René Descartes, Thomas Edison, Johann Wolfgang von Goethe, Steve Jobs, John Stuart Mill, Plato, Tupac Shakur, Leonardo da Vinci, Swami Vivekananda, Orville and Wilbur Wright.

Description of the Principle

Perhaps you feel that you are prepared and ready to unleash your genius to the world. Not so fast. It is good to have ambition, but it is even more important to have the right foundation necessary to nurture the genius mind. You may be aware that brilliant people are often good at making connections between many topics. Understand that this ability requires having a basic amount of knowledge in order to help see such connections. The best thing you can do is build up a foundation of knowledge early in life. This can be accomplished through formal schooling, reading, discussions with learned people, or in other ways. There is no single correct path. Ideally, you would combine book learning and practical hands-on learning.

In this foundational learning phase, the goal is to attain a broad understanding of a variety of fields. Your studies may include history, philosophy, mathematics, art, and science, among many other topics. Don't expect to become a leader of any field while building your foundation. For many, this will be a period of self-discovery, of finding what you truly want to focus on in life. But it is important not to jump ahead too fast. If you fail to grasp the fundamentals early on, you will just be playing catch-up later on.

Realize that there can be danger in knowing only one thing, even if you know it very well. Many occupations require a broad range of knowledge, for one thing. Also, if you over-focus on one topic, you may set yourself up for making silly mistakes. A scientist may get excited, feeling that he is on the verge of the greatest discovery of humankind. But if he only knew the history of his profession, he would realize this discovery was already made 80 years ago, and found 15 years later to be incorrect. History is a particularly good example of a topic to gain some familiarity with, because as Edmund Burke said, "Those who don't know history are doomed to repeat it."

Benefits of the Principle

Having a solid foundation, and an understanding of many different disciplines, will help your creative ability. Often, creative breakthroughs are made by an epiphany of realizing that one topic has a relationship to another. These relationships can be in completely different domains. As a fictional example, in the TV series *House*, Dr. House (played by actor Hugh Laurie) frequently solves a medical emergency where someone's life is in danger. And he will do this while engaged in a random conversation that appears to have nothing to do with the medical case. He has such a broad range of knowledge that he is able to connect ideas many other people would have missed. Even though this is a fictional example, it is still a valid point. Building a solid foundation can help with creativity and with finding interesting and unique solutions to problems.

The broader and more firm your foundation is, the more you will begin to see patterns and connections across even areas that seem completely unrelated. And in large part, geniuses are people who see more patterns and connections than most people. Part of the reason they can do this is because of their strong foundation of knowledge. In seeing more patterns and connections, you will be more likely to make more advances in your field than your peers. A common mistake is to think that the foundation is unimportant, and loaded with irrelevant information. It is risky to think in this way. Actually, all information can become relevant at unexpected times. For example, Steve Jobs took a calligraphy course (e.g., on artistic or stylized handwriting) which he credits as being important to the design of Apple computers. In a 2005 commencement speech he gave at Stanford, he said:

If I had never dropped out [of college], I would have never dropped in on this calligraphy class, and personal computers might not have the wonderful typography

that they do. Of course, it was impossible to connect
the dots looking forward when I was in college. But it
was very, very clear looking backwards ten years later.

Learning calligraphy may seem completely irrelevant to
running a company that builds computers, but it wasn't. Don't
think your foundation needs to be boring. You can choose for
yourself what you want to learn in building your foundation.
Just remember that the benefits will be greatest when you are
open to learning many topics.

As another example of the benefits of a strong foundation,
consider Ben Carson. He was an African American boy who
grew up in a Detroit ghetto. In *Gifted Hands: The Ben Carson
Story* (referring to the book, but there is a movie of the same
title based on the book) we learn that as a child, his grades were
the worst in his class. Other children would tease him, calling
him "dummy" or other names. Around this point, the situation
seemed hopeless, and even Ben himself started to believe that
perhaps he was dumb. Then things started to change. His mother,
who only had a third grade education herself, started cleaning
for people who were generally wealthy and well-educated. And
she noticed that many of these people read books. With the fact
that Ben and her other son Curtis were underperforming, she
knew what she had to do:

> *Mother had already decided how we would spend our*
> *free time when we weren't watching television. "You*
> *boys are going to go to the library and check out books.*
> *You're going to read at least two books every week. At*
> *the end of each week you'll give me a report on what*
> *you've read."*

At first, the boys couldn't believe it. It seemed impossible to
read even one book in a week. Neither had ever read a book on
their own, aside from what was required for school assignments.

Nonetheless, they respected their mother and did as she told them. Their mother's decision quickly became a turning point for Ben (and his brother too). Gradually, Ben moved from being one of the worst students at his school as a child, to being one of the brightest students by the time he was in high school. Although most students of his upbringing were not even eligible to go to a major university, Ben was accepted into Yale with a scholarship. He eventually became a neurosurgeon and gained notoriety for performing difficult surgeries that were declined by most other surgeons. And he performed them successfully.

The decision to have Ben read instead of watching television in his free time, changed the course of his life. He went from the worst student, to one of the best. He probably read more than almost any other student, and so his foundation was firmly established. Dr. Ben Carson's life is an excellent example of how we all have the ability to build our foundation and change everything around, even if you start off at a disadvantage in life.

How to Apply the Principle

Learn from a broad range of resources

The best time to establish a firm foundation is when you are young, but it is never too late to start. To build a foundation, take in your information from a broad range of sources. This may include books, articles, films, museums, classes, travels to new places, and so forth. Don't feel limited to these, either. Broaden your education by broadening the sources of information that you go to.

Learn in topics that interrelate with many others

In choosing what to learn as a part of your foundation, put more consideration in topics that interrelate with many others. Some examples of this would be history, mathematics, psychology, geography, music, languages, general science, literature, and art. You will find that knowledge in topics such as these can be highly valuable, because it tends to relate to many other areas. For example, psychology is the study of human behavior. Understanding psychology can apply to learning about people in history, consumer behavior in a business, and also it can relate to criminal cases that happen in society, since they are committed by human beings, to name a few.

Make friends who are experts in a variety of fields

Make friends and acquaintances with people who study and practice in a wide range of professions and activities. Ask them about their work, what they do in a normal day, and what kind of insights they have come to in their field. It can be useful to ask about common misconceptions people have about what they do. Learning in this way can offer you a break from more intense forms of learning, such as studying textbooks.

Secret Principle #12: **Depth**

Gain a Depth of Knowledge

"A man cannot understand the art he is studying if he only looks for the end result without taking the time to delve deeply into the reasoning of the study."

— **Miyamoto Musashi** was an expert Japanese swordsman and rōnin, with an undefeated record in his 60 duels, many of them to the death.

Geniuses Who Applied the Principle

Marie Curie, Charles Darwin, Albert Einstein, Miyamoto Musashi, Isaac Newton, Sakichi Toyoda, Leonardo da Vinci.

Description of the Principle

Most brilliant people become known for their knowledge and discoveries in one specific field. Usually, they have acquired such an extensive knowledge in one area that they end up becoming a leading expert. As important as it is to gain a solid foundation (and a breadth of knowledge), and be able to tie in important ideas from different areas, it is also important to learn something at great depth. You should desire to become a master in a domain and to know it better than anyone else.

When you pursue greater depths of knowledge, this means you will learn all of the main parts of a larger field. For example, if you decide to focus on physics, as you gain in depth knowledge, you will develop a solid understanding of mathematics, especially in equations that deal with physics, along with weak forces, strong forces, gravity, and electromagnetism. These are all areas that would require careful study, but if you choose to learn about physics at depth, it will be important to know them. Keep in mind that often, experts will choose a subspecialty and focus completely on it. For example, Einstein focused on problems dealing with time, the speed of light, and relativity.

It is not practical to pursue the path of genius, and to only pursue a moderate amount of knowledge on various topics. Some brilliant people are able to learn many fields deeply, especially if they are somewhat related, such as mathematics, chemistry, and physics. Fewer will learn completely unrelated fields at great depth, but it does sometimes happen, as with Goethe and da Vinci. To have the best chance on your path to genius, you should pursue both breadth and depth of knowledge. In most cases, it will make sense to build up your foundation (or breadth of knowledge) first, and then to specialize in one particular thing you are most interested and motivated in.

Benefits of the Principle

One well-known genius who went to great depths of understanding was Leonardo da Vinci. He had the mindset of delving deeper into everything he did. In order to become a better painter, he wasn't satisfied in simply understanding the human body at skin depth. In fact, he did something many of us would find grotesque, but he did it to understand the human body more deeply. Da Vinci would dissect human cadavers. He wanted to know how the bones, organs, and internal workings were arranged beneath the skin. He believed this greater understanding of the human body as a whole would make him a better painter, and it did. Observers of his work have often sensed that his paintings appear to come to life.

Learning deeply is the essence of where true genius ability comes from. Brilliant minds tend to become fascinated with a topic, and this fascination makes them want to know everything they can about the area. It isn't enough to learn superficial facts. They must truly understand it inside and out. When you have acquired such a deep understanding of something, it will be easier for you to learn new things in your field. You will already know the main principles and ideas in your area of focus, and you will quickly see how new information ties into what you have already learned.

The leaders of a field often have the most knowledge in an area. But it isn't just the amount of knowledge they have that makes them special. Typically, they will have a very deep amount of knowledge in something specific. They will know more about this area than anyone else. Acquiring a deeper knowledge will help you to position yourself as a leader in your field. As a leader, you would have more control over your work, and have more freedom to advance in your progress.

How to Apply the Principle

Five Whys

This is a technique of asking questions to get to the deeper root of a problem. It can also be used to gain a greater understanding of a topic. It was first used by Sakichi Toyoda within the Toyota Motor Company. The technique involves asking "Why" five times, each time gaining a deeper understanding of the true problem.

As an example, if you are studying global warming, you might ask these questions and get the following answers:

Why is global warming happening?

Because the Earth is getting warmer.

Why is it getting warmer?

Because the Earth is absorbing more heat from the Sun than it used to.

Why is the Earth absorbing more heat?

Because there is more carbon dioxide in the atmosphere.

Why is there more carbon dioxide?

There are some natural reasons for carbon dioxide, but much of the increase is because of people.

Why are people increasing the carbon dioxide?

People use power plants, cars, planes, and other industrial facilities which introduce more carbon into the air, which warms up the Earth on average. This last solution gets at the true reason global warming is happening.

As you can see, asking "Why" several times (it doesn't need to be exactly five) can help you learn more and more deeply about a topic. Of course, you may need to look up some answers on your own, or ask an expert, but this will help advance your knowledge and understanding.

Formal studies

One of the more typical paths to building a deeper understanding is to undergo a formal plan of study. You may earn a degree, such as a Bachelors, Masters, or PhD, or go through a certificate program. With this approach you will learn from professors or instructors who are experts in your field. Keep in mind that to gain a true depth of understanding can take many years, and even be a lifelong quest. For example, someone with a PhD will know a topic the most deeply, but will also have spent the greatest amount of time acquiring knowledge in their specialization.

Informal studies

A depth of knowledge can also be gained through informal studies, such as through books, online courses and instructional materials, interviewing experts, and so forth. You won't have a formal instructional program, but if you are dedicated and patient, you can still learn a great deal on your own. The way you go about pursuing a depth of knowledge will depend on your goals. Some careers will require a degree, and others may not.

If you are studying on your own, you will want to be sure to learn from a variety of experts. Keep in mind that there is rarely one authoritative resource that can tell you everything you need to know. And often, experts will disagree with each other. You will advance more deeply in your understanding when you question the experts, compare their opinions against each other, and build your own independent understanding based on critical thinking.

Secret Principle #13: **Notes**

Take Detailed Notes

"Keep a notebook. Travel with it, eat with it, sleep with it. Slap into it every stray thought that flutters up into your brain. Cheap paper is less perishable than gray matter, and lead pencil markings endure longer than memory."

— **Jack London**, American novelist, journalist, and social activist.

Geniuses Who Applied the Principle

Aristotle, Charles Darwin, Michael Faraday, Victor Hugo, Jack London, Isaac Newton, Marcel Proust, Srinivasa Ramanujan, Oliver Sacks, Leonardo da Vinci.

Description of the Principle

Taking notes can seem tedious, but many great minds have been practically obsessive about documenting the things they found important. This makes sense, as the best way to be sure you'll remember something and be able to use it later is to record it. This isn't just something done by students. You will find it useful to keep good notes so you can examine them at a later time and think about them more thoroughly. Perhaps with time you will come to understand them in a new way, or more deeply.

There are many reasons to take notes, depending on your goals. If you are an artist, you may draw sketches or outlines of things you find especially interesting. Perhaps you can build those sketches up into a larger project later. If you are a novelist, you may write down interesting conversations you overhear. Perhaps you can work these ideas into your novel later. For the inventor, it could be a good idea to write down any time you are frustrated with a design. You may be able to improve upon it later.

Benefits of the Principle

Victor Hugo, the author of *Les Miserables*, the *Hunchback of Notre Dame*, and other works, carried little notebooks everywhere he went. According to *Daily Rituals* by Mason Currey, he was known to write down virtually everything he said, along with the responses of those around him. He found it important to document everything he could, because it might end up being something valuable he could use in a book. With the great works he created, evidently his detailed notes were quite helpful.

Brilliant minds will not be satisfied to remain at the same level of understanding, or at the same level of progress, for too long. Taking notes on what works, what doesn't work, unexpected results, and so forth, is a good start toward making progress. If you commit to taking detailed notes, you will position yourself to grow and expand in your abilities.

How to Apply the Principle

Always have a notepad or notetaking device ready

You never know when ideas will strike. They often come at unexpected times, so you have to be prepared. They may come when you are staring into the sea, watching television, or of course, when you purposely make the time to brainstorm. If you don't have a way to keep notes at all times, you will risk losing your best ideas. Perhaps this is why some of the most brilliant geniuses were so obsessive about note-taking. They understood that it was an unacceptable risk, to potentially lose a breakthrough idea forever. Sometimes, in a moment of inspiration, many ideas will come to mind all at once in a frenzy. If you don't write them down fast, it is easy to lose them.

Consider using different devices and systems for notetaking

With today's technology, there are numerous ways to take notes. You can use pencil and paper, a computer, a smartphone, or even an audio recorder. Take your notes as you think of them or observe them, and evaluate later on if they were important or useful. It's easy to make the mistake of getting an idea, and to either think it is brilliant when it is not, or that it is an awful idea when it is actually good. Take notes first, and evaluate later.

Focus on the important things

Take notes on things related to your most important goals. If you want to be a storywriter for films, take notes on your favorite films. You could take notes on story structure, things you like about the setting, the characters, etc. Through this kind of study and documentation, you will improve in your skills.

If you want to rise to the level of executive in your company, take notes about the executives you admire and respect. How do they handle difficult problems? How do they interact with subordinates? What kind of words do they use?

Be open to more types of notetaking than just writing

Keep in mind that you can take notes in many different forms. Of course there are written notes, but there are also concept maps, timelines, outlines, drawings or sketches, diagrams (such as Venn Diagrams), and so forth. Don't limit yourself to just words and sentences, if you find that you think best in other ways. Also, you have to consider the system that makes the most sense depending on your subject matter.

Secret Principle #14: **Master**

Take the Path of Great Masters

"It is a mistake to think that the practice of my art has become easy to me. I assure you, dear friend, no one has given so much care to the study of composition as I. There is scarcely a famous master in music whose works I have not frequently and diligently studied."

— **Wolfgang Amadeus Mozart,** prolific and influential musical composer of the Classical era.

Geniuses Who Applied the Principle

The Beatles, Michael Faraday, Benjamin Franklin, John Keats, Wolfgang Amadeus Mozart, Pablo Picasso.

Description of the Principle

In the medieval ages it was common for young workers to go through an apprenticeship. Today, we often receive training, sometimes on the job itself, or we go to an institution of higher learning. Under the apprentice system, a young worker would start as a complete beginner, and hope to learn all the fundamentals of the craft from a master. The process could take around seven years. At the end, the worker would have to prove his skills and abilities in order to pass onto the next level, journeyman.

The apprenticeship was an effective and practical way to learn, and is still used today. To learn from the masters doesn't necessarily mean you must go through a formal apprenticeship. Rather, the point is to realize that masters have been through the process of being a beginner and they have already proven themselves. The master knows the most important tasks that must be done in your field. The novice can easily become overwhelmed through lack of experience, but with guidance everything is much more manageable.

Benefits of the Principle

Wolfgang Amadeus Mozart was obviously highly talented. From a young age, he loved to play the piano. But what is easily forgotten is that he had a father who was a talented composer and musician in his own right, Leopold Mozart. According to the Mozart.com article "Mozart and his Father", "Wolfgang Amadeus Mozart was tremendously lucky to have an experienced musician as a father with Leopold Mozart. Leopold immediately recognized the potential in Wolfgang. He dedicated his life to supporting his son's talent."

His father was there to help the young Mozart by giving him appropriate songs to play for his level, to help with technique, and with giving feedback to help him improve. With many of the most talented geniuses, their talent is so great that the masters they worked under can be easily forgotten. However, the guidance they receive is often a key component to the progress of the brilliant mind. Consider that someone had to teach the young Mozart how to read sheet music, which is its own kind of musical language. The fact that he learned everything fluidly and enjoyed the whole process can make it seem like the master, his father, had little impact. But without him, Mozart couldn't have made as much progress as he did.

In many fields, you need access to certain resources to be able to work. In music, you need an instrument or studio equipment. In statistics, you need the right computer programs. In agronomy, you need arable land (e.g., suitable for planting) and an irrigation system. The master, of course, is much more likely to have access to the relevant resources than a complete novice would. If you are just starting out, it is important to find the right master who not only has the resources you need, but is willing to allow you to use at least some of them. The other perk is that the master may be able to give you tips as to how you can acquire your own resources.

One of the most important benefits of finding the right master, is that he will probably know where the work is. If you are in a field where jobs are scarce, a master will be quite good at finding work. In fact, he is probably good enough that people are calling him to ask for his services. On the other hand, the novice often has great trouble acquiring work. But you may find a good partnership with the right master. You can provide work for free or cheap, and gain immense experience. Also, you can learn how to best find new work while building a reputation for yourself.

How to Apply the Principle

Find a master

You will want to find a master in your chosen field. You can search online or locally. The most likely way to draw interest is if you volunteer to work for free. If you can't afford to work for free, keep in mind that you could offer to do this part-time.

When you do this, you will stand to learn a great deal directly from a master. This is one of the most effective ways to learn, which is why the apprenticeship system was popular even in the medieval ages. Search for a master that fits with your needs. First, is the master an expert in what you specifically want to learn? Look for one who is accomplishing the things you would like to accomplish one day. As you assist them in their work, you can gain insights you wouldn't have otherwise had. And in time you should feel confident and expert enough to venture off on your own.

Mimic the master

Many of us want to be unique, original, and stand out (as in Principle #6). However, when we are just starting to learn, it can be a better option to understand how the great masters of the past have worked. In fact, an excellent way to learn can be through mimicry, or by emulating the master. As a form of practice, it will be helpful to learn to do as the master does, very closely, perhaps even identically. For example, some novelists have practiced writing good novels by simply rewriting out famous novels, such as Ernest Hemingway's works. If you prefer not to copy identically, you may change the sentence structure but keep the message the same. The point is that going through the process that a master did helps to internalize it so that it can be called to action at a later time. As another example, a painter may try to recreate the same exact work that a master created. Any errors will be a great chance for the master to teach the student a lesson in technique. Do not confuse these acts with plagiarism or forgery. The above recommendations are a training technique, and not intended for anyone to pass off someone else's work as their own.

Seek multiple mentors

Rather than choose one master, you may go with the option of having multiple masters that you look up to as mentors. You could try to befriend them and ask questions. Let them know that you would like to learn more from them, and ask if they have time to discuss a specific concept or process. Don't take up too much of their time all at once. Recall that this would be a favor. You can always approach different masters on your own. They may include experts, executives, or professors, for example.

To start, figure out where they tend to be that you would also be welcome. This may be through online groups or at a conference. Do these masters have a blog you can visit and leave comments on, possibly allowing you to gain some attention? Do they give presentations at the University that you may be able to attend? Get involved with the same kind of tasks and venues that they take part in, and you will increase your chance of making a meaningful connection.

Follow the media of masters

Lastly, if you feel that the masters are out of your reach, for any reason, there is another way to gain access to them. You can always seek out great masters, their ideas, and their wisdom through the media that they have worked on. The ideas or works of many masters are captured in media, either through books, articles, audio recordings, videos, or other formats. Sometimes these materials will cost, and other times they may be free. It can be especially helpful to pinpoint one master who you look up to, and to consume all of the media the person has available. Learn everything you can in this way, for it will be the cheapest education you can receive at the highest value. The best places to access such works will be online, through libraries, or museums.

Secret Principle #15: **Classics**

Value the Classics and Use Them to Explore Great Minds

"Classics are books which, the more we think we know them through hearsay, the more original, unexpected, and innovative we find them when we actually read them."

— **Italo Calvino,** Italian journalist and writer of short stories and novels.

Geniuses Who Applied the Principle

Jorge Luis Borges, Italo Calvino, Johann Wolfgang von Goethe, John Stuart Mill, William Shakespeare, Mark Zuckerberg.

Description of the Principle

Classics are books or other works of various kinds that have stood the test of time. The mass public has endorsed them time and time again for their beauty, usefulness, or historic value. These have become the classics, known and revered, usually with good reason.

There are many different types of classics, and in many different fields. There are books, movies, music, architecture, sculptures, philosophical works, ancient artwork, etc. In movies, there are the works of Alfred Hitchcock and Stanley Kubrick. In artwork, there is Frida Kahlo and Vincent van Gogh. In literature, there is Miguel de Cervantes and Isaac Asimov. In theater, there is Sophocles and Shakespeare. In nonfiction, there is Sun Tzu's *The Art of War*, and Niccolo Machiavelli's *The Prince*. In music, there are the works of Wolfgang Amadeus Mozart and Franz Liszt. These are just a few examples. Really, the classics are very broad, and will differ depending on who you ask, the time period, and your location. They can also be from as recent as twenty years ago to as distant as thousands of years in the past.

Benefits of the Principle

John Stuart Mill was learning Greek at three years old, and Latin at eight years old. By 14, he knew the Greek and Latin classics quite well. This education was a part of his foundation (Principle #11). Given the emphasis placed on him learning the classics in his childhood, it is clear that they influenced his development and his understanding of his place in the world. Certainly it played a role in his thinking. These are all important things, considering he ultimately became one of the most influential English philosophers. It isn't always clear exactly how exposure to the classics will help us. But they have often been critical to the development of the great masters of history.

Keep in mind, that with classical works you are able to experience the highest level of quality from ages past. You get to enter into a time portal and visit and experience the best work from the greatest masters throughout history. This can be an excellent way to familiarize yourself with the past works in your own field, or to complement your knowledge with the classical works in other fields.

The classics can show you a different way of thinking, or a different process from the norm, which can help spark new ideas. Sometimes, we get used to hearing about the same ideas and perspectives, perhaps because we often associate with people similar to ourselves (e.g., same socioeconomic status, geography, language, and culture). Reach for a classic, and this will allow you to experience a different time period, culture, and a new way of looking at the world. This will in turn help you to gain new insights.

How to Apply the Principle

Identify and read or consume the classics in your field

Whatever industry or field you wish to master, make time to learn some of the classical works in the area. There are different classics specific to each field. You can identify them because they are usually older, and they may be mentioned or cited frequently, but not necessarily read or experienced widely. We often come to rely on either summaries, hearsay, or newer works which were likely inspired or influenced by the classics. But it can be the most useful and practical to read or expose yourself to the classics directly. For example, for the scientist, it could make a lot of sense to read Charles Darwin's *On the Origin of Species* to learn his firsthand account of how evolution works. Of course, the concept of evolution itself has changed or evolved in time, but it can still be useful to understand what evidence he found that led him on the path to discovering evolution.

Sometimes the classics may appear dull, outdated, or even irrelevant, but it is a mistake to discount them so easily. The ancient Greeks, even thousands of years ago, were great thinkers, and made discoveries which helped pave the way to modern science and philosophical thought. For instance, *The*

Republic by Plato is one of the world's most influential works of philosophy and political theory, and has stood the test of time for millennia. Do not assume that you cannot learn something from great thinkers of ages past. You may be surprised.

Secret Principle #16: **Experience**

Pursue Experiences that Offer the Greatest Learning

"It's a terrible thing, I think, in life to wait until you're ready. I have this feeling now that actually no one is ever ready to do anything. There is almost no such thing as ready. There is only now. And you may as well do it now. Generally speaking, now is as good a time as any."

— **Hugh Laurie,** English actor, writer, director, musician, singer, comedian, and author.

Geniuses Who Applied the Principle

Albert Einstein, Michael Faraday, Benjamin Franklin, Leonardo da Vinci.

Description of the Principle

First, I want to clarify that I like the Hugh Laurie quote above because the greatest opportunity for learning is often in doing things you feel you are not yet ready for. By the time you feel ready, the opportunity may be gone, never to return. We have to be willing to learn on the spot, to be a keen observer and use all of our attention to improve as we go. Sometimes all of this is under the pressure that a failure can result in losing a job or big opportunity, but we must use that pressure to push ourselves to do even better. Under such circumstances, we will have to work harder than everyone else to show that we are worthy of the work, and willing to learn anything necessary to perform at the highest level.

Understand that when given the option, brilliant minds will tend to go for the one where they can learn the most. Even if there is fear, anxiety, or uncertainty in their abilities, they will tend to pursue the path that offers the most learning. If necessary, they will sacrifice time and money to gain the knowledge which is important to them. For instance, Einstein worked as a patent clerk for eight years because it gave him the time to focus on his true passion, physics. If he had been focused on a job with a greater reputation or income, he may have never had his brilliant discoveries in physics.

Geniuses are not passive in how they go about learning new things. They don't wait for someone to knock on their door with an opportunity for learning. Instead, they actively seek out the best opportunities. Their tendency to be active in their learning can be seen through many other principles in this book. They gain a foundation of knowledge (Principle #11), take detailed notes (Principle #13), and seek masters (Principle #14), for example. They want to learn all that they can, and not leave it up to chance.

Benefits of the Principle

The key benefit is simple. When you take the path toward the greatest learning, you will learn much more in less time. This means you will be able to make more progress and advance further in your field. If you repeat the process of always selecting the paths that present greater learning, or even creating those paths for yourself, your expertise and mastery will rise much faster than if you simply took the most convenient path.

And having this greater expertise will allow you to put your focus on bigger and tougher problems. You won't need to struggle to understand fundamental concepts because through being in the habit of taking the path of greater learning, you will quickly master them. You will find yourself gravitating toward bigger and bigger challenges. Perhaps you will fail at a task occasionally, but you will learn from these events and be better prepared to succeed the next time around. You will always be making progress and never remain stagnant in your abilities.

By seeking the greatest learning opportunities, you will find that as you perform well at some of your endeavors, new opportunities will open up for you. People will come to understand that you are a serious learner, and in time your ability to learn will itself grow and evolve. You will be highly valued for your ability to understand new things quickly and to make smooth transitions into different areas. In time, you will find the best opportunities will tend to open up to you first.

How to Apply the Principle

Take the challenging path

What will the path toward the greatest learning look like? Usually it will be especially challenging. You may feel uncomfortable, and uncertain if you are even ready to proceed. This is why your foundation (Principle #11) is incredibly important. If you know the fundamentals, learning new things won't be as difficult as you imagine. The computer technician who has learned how to use twenty programs shouldn't be concerned about needing to learn one or two new ones, for example. All of the background knowledge he has of other programs will help him learn new programs much more efficiently.

Ask: Which option is a better learning opportunity?

Any time you are presented with new options or opportunities, ask yourself which one will allow you to learn the most. This approach will be most important in your youth, when you have more to learn, and you can afford to sacrifice income in the short-term in order to gain understanding. In time, your complete mastery will help you to earn the income you desire. Also, when presented with opportunities, ask yourself which one will allow you to learn what is most important to you? Perhaps you are eager to be in a position of leadership. Then it would be wise to seek positions that allow a chance to have any form of leadership over others, even if you would not be officially ranked as a superior.

Try many positions

Make an effort to try every position that you can in your line of work. Many of us will become comfortable after being in a position for a long time. But this can be dangerous. You may know one thing well, but what if a critical member of your team decides to quit and you need to learn how to do their job right away? It is obviously preferable to understand how your work connects to other people's work before something like this happens. You may be surprised that some jobs or task which seem difficult are actually fairly straightforward to learn. You may even discover a new talent in the process. There is no need to stray from your assigned tasks at your work. But if you finish them early, if it is a slow day, or if someone needs extra help, you can volunteer to help someone else.

Keep an opportunistic mindset

Generally, have an opportunistic and open mindset. If an acquaintance mentions that she is enrolling in a pottery course, offer to join her. If you sit next to a chef on a plane, try to learn some secrets to cooking great tasting food. If a friend is working on an invention, but you are the expert in the area and he is not, offer some helpful suggestions. Do not rule out learning opportunities offhand. Give it a try, and see where it goes.

Secret Principle #17: Connections

Build Connections

"Study the science of art. Study the art of science. Develop your senses – especially learn how to see. Realize that everything connects to everything else."

— **Leonardo da Vinci,** Italian polymath whose areas of interest included invention, painting, sculpture, architecture, science, music, mathematics, engineering, literature, anatomy, geology, astronomy, botany, writing, history, poetry, and cartography.

Geniuses Who Applied the Principle

Albert Einstein, Michael Faraday, Johann Wolfgang von Goethe, Christopher Langan, Leonardo da Vinci.

Description of the Principle

It is probably no coincidence that some of the brightest people who worked in many fields, such as Johann von Goethe and Leonardo da Vinci, were the ones who emphasized that they saw many interconnections between topics. Many of us get used to fitting topics neatly into different areas, inside our minds. But those brilliant people who made an effort to see interconnections between practically everything, may help us see that perhaps there are no distinct lines that separate math from science, science from art, or art from history.

This principle of connection, will line up most directly with the way our brains actually work. The brain itself is one big network of interconnected neurons. It only makes sense that building connections would be a principle of genius. We all make connections, of course, but brilliant minds will make it a point to seek out more and more of them. They want to know how one thing relates to another. But they aren't satisfied there. They want to see how everything relates to every other thing.

Some brilliant minds have actually been interested in taking connections a step further, and searching for a great unity in their field. Albert Einstein, for example, wanted to find a unifying theory that could unite the rules of physics both on a small scale (e.g., quantum physics) and a large scale (e.g., classical physics). He was searching for a principle that connected both, which would have changed the way everyone viewed physics. This was perhaps one of the most ambitious undertakings in scientific history. Even he knew the odds were stacked against him. He never did find this unifying theory, but the fact that he was interested in it shows how important connections were to him.

As another example, consider Christopher Langan. He has a reported IQ from 190-210 (although note that scores becomes less reliable at these high ranges) and has been described by the media as "the smartest man in America". Langan has connected many different areas with his Cognitive Theoretic Model of the Universe. The main components are actually in the title itself: cognitive theory, modeling, and the universe itself. In an interview on Superscholar.org, he was asked to describe the theory in plain English. Part of his response was:

Cognitive theory refers to a general language of cognition (the structural and transitional rules of cognition); universe refers to the content of that language, or that to which the language refers; and model refers to the mapping which carries the content into the language, thus creating information.

He has also said "you cannot describe the universe completely with any accuracy unless you're willing to admit that it's both physical and mental in nature". Langan has worked on this "theory of the relationship between mind and reality" for decades, where clearly he has made connections that many of us might not have intuitively made (e.g., mind, universe, modeling, language). The theory is described in more detail at CTMU.org

Benefits of the Principle

Challenging yourself to make connections between different fields can help improve your creative ability. Often, when there is a big problem, people become locked into seeing it in just one way. They have a difficult time changing how they look at it, and struggle to make much progress in solving it. When you can connect one problem with something else, even if it appears unrelated at first, you will greatly increase your chance of finding good solutions. Your ability to see areas as related, when others see them as completely separate, will also help you to make creative breakthroughs and perceive links other people had not noticed.

If you were to focus on understanding how everything interconnects, even seemingly unconnected areas, you could learn about a variety of topics at depth, all at once. Many people will get confused when they try to learn too many different subjects at one time, because they will not see a relationship or connection. But if you practice understanding the interrelationships, you will position yourself to master a variety of unique fields, as Johann von Goethe and Leonardo da Vinci did.

How to Apply the Principle

How does your field connect with related areas?

To make more connections, ask yourself how one topic relates to many others. For example, it is clear that mathematics interrelates with chemistry, physics, computer science, and statistics. Business interrelates with economics, statistics, communication, law, and psychology. Geography relates to history, sociology, anthropology, and meteorology. To get started with making connections, ask yourself how your field or fields of interest connect closely to others. Learn those relationships and connections as deeply as you can. Then take things a step further. Start asking yourself how your field may connect to areas that seem completely unrelated. For example, a farmer may have something to teach you about parenting. He may tell you that to plant a seed and abandon it is silly. He would tell you it requires sunlight, water, fertilizer, and ongoing monitoring to make sure it is progressing well. Similarly, a child cannot be expected to do well if left alone. She needs food, water, guidance, and ongoing monitoring to make sure she is progressing well.

Look for relationships between things that appear unrelated

Stretch your ability to make connections. Start asking how even things that seem completely unrelated and disconnected, could in fact be connected. For example, how does the political system of the ancient Greeks relate to the political systems today? How does the flight of birds relate to the flight of commercial planes? How does the social structure of ants relate to the social structure of humans? Notice that in most of these examples something that you are probably less familiar with was compared to something that you are likely more familiar with. Keep in mind that connections are easier to make when you are working with some familiarity with at least one of the ideas. You can come up with more questions like this for yourself, and then search for the relationships.

Thinking, Strategies,
Problem-Solving

"First and last, what is demanded of genius is love of truth."

– Johann Wolfgang von Goethe, German writer and statesman, with works of poetry and fiction, and treatises on botany, anatomy, and color.

Hopefully you can see that the right personal qualities and dedication to learning are both very important to building a brilliant mind. You can think of the prior two sections as providing the necessary conditions for genius to arise. And now that you are ready, this section will be a bit more advanced and elaborate.

The way geniuses think, their strategies and approaches to making sense of the world, and how they solve problems are all intertwined, and so they will all be covered in this section.

The reality is that how geniuses think is not so easy to discover. There is no straightforward way to get inside the greatest minds who ever lived. Of course, since we do not have access to their minds, we must look at their actions, their words, and even their creations in order to gain a clue as to what went on inside. This section will cover thinking patterns that these bright minds went through, in light of this kind of evidence.

We will also look at strategies they used for understanding the world around them. Brilliant minds are superb at coming up with useful systems, approaches, and strategies to quickly make sense of the world. The wonderful thing is that these can be learned and practiced, even by those of us who do not yet consider ourselves geniuses.

Another important aspect of great minds is how they solve problems. There are many types of problems, of course, but there are some ways in which they are all similar, and brilliant minds have specific approaches that they bring to virtually all problems. We will learn this, so we too can be better problem-solvers.

Question and Test Your Assumptions

"If we all worked on the assumption that what is accepted as true is really true, there would be little hope of advance."

— Orville Wright, American inventor and aviation pioneer.

Geniuses Who Applied the Principle

Isaac Asimov, Charles Darwin, Albert Einstein, Bertrand Russell, Mark Twain, Orville and Wilbur Wright.

Description of the Principle

You may have heard the advice, "Don't make assumptions". When you think about it though, this is not practical advice. Instead, it makes more sense to question and test your assumptions.

For example, every day, as a matter of being human and living our lives, we *must* make assumptions. I assume that when I get up in the morning all of my furniture and items will be in the same places as I left them when I went to sleep the night before. I also assume the floor will not break underneath me when I walk on wood, carpet, or marble. These scenarios are so consistently predictable that you probably make these assumptions too. Most of us are probably aware that we need to be careful about assuming too much, but you must understand that no matter how much we try to avoid making assumptions, we will always have to make some.

With that said, it is still important to question many assumptions. For example, often a respected person or leader will make a statement, and many people will repeat it as if it were a fact. And a repeated assumption is made, as word spreads and everyone assumes that the message is accurate. Instead, we should be cautious about accepting something as fact too quickly. Of course, questioning assumptions will become more critical when you are planning to take action based on the information you receive. To take action based on a faulty assumption can result in big errors, so we must be careful to avoid this.

Benefits of the Principle

When you question the assumptions of others, and even your own, you will help to stop yourself from wasting time and losing productivity. By catching one faulty assumption and stopping yourself from moving in that direction, you will be able to make steady progress instead of getting stuck. Keep in mind that even if you believe in one wrong assumption, it will be easy to make even more incorrect assumptions. For example, if I tell you the Earth is flat, and you believe it, it's easy to think all planets are flat and the sun too. One bad assumption can lead to many more. Instead, the genius tends to be good at finding the best intellectual paths to explore. One way of doing this is actually to eliminate the bad paths that lead nowhere, the false assumptions.

Let's look at a problem with accepting too many assumptions without questioning them. When people believe in a bad assumption, they tend to stop looking for alternative explanations. There have been many times in history, and recent times when even scientists have made incorrect assumptions. Sometimes they may have been so eager to make progress that they did not take the time to make sure their assumptions were all valid. In many cases, this led to years or even decades without progress. What is worse, is there is often a chain reaction of several scientists or people believing an assumption. After enough people believe in it, it becomes "common knowledge", and people seem even less likely to question it. The lesson is clear: We need to question assumptions and test them for ourselves, even those that may be accepted by the majority.

If you want to observe many assumptions at work, observe children. As children, we tend to make a variety of assumptions, which some of us even carry into adulthood. As a young child (e.g., around nine years and younger) I made a type of assumption that other children might make too. I assumed everything was as it appeared to be. Everything people told me was always true, without exception. Every rule that I learned always applied, every single time without fail. I can actually recall the exact moment that shattered this pattern of assumption making for me. I was in Chicago, walking ahead of my mother through the city. There was a "Do not walk" sign, so I stopped. A moment later the sign switched to "Walk", and so I started to walk forward. Through the corner of my eye I saw something moving fast, so I stopped. It was a car running the red light. My movement was enough to scare the driver, who slammed on the breaks. His wheels landed about a foot in front of me. I took a step back, and he apologized and drove on. My mother rushed forward and I told her that the sign said "Walk". She said "Yes, I know, but sometimes people don't follow the rules. You have to be careful." Clearly, we have to be cautious about assuming a rule or concept will *always* apply.

How to Apply the Principle

Just because you hear it often, doesn't make it true

Sometimes, we see or hear one 'fact' in so many different places, that it begins to seem true. Have you heard that we only use 10% of our brains? This is something stated frequently, probably by people who assumed that it was true when they heard it, but it is not a fact. This is not a statement that can be supported scientifically. How easily these so-called facts become part of mainstream knowledge can be scary. Consider that surely everything stated in ads and commercials can't be 100% true. But we may hear certain things so often that we believe them to be true, just through the repetition. Be cautious with this. Avoid thinking that just because you have heard something many times that it must be true.

Know where your information is coming from

Stop and ask yourself where your information is coming from. This may be an interesting point to use your author, myself, as an example. Your source of information in this book is coming from someone with a Bachelor's degree in psychology from Purdue University, and a Master's degree in industrial-organizational psychology from the University of Oklahoma. I have written many academic articles and popular books about intellectual and creative abilities.

The point is you should have some awareness of where your information is coming from. If you can't trust the source, or if your source is not an expert in the area that they give advice, then you can't trust the information. Knowing your source of information will help prevent you from making poor assumptions. Obviously, you should not trust your barber with advice about your health. But you can probably trust your family physician with this.

Of course even when your information is coming from a trusted expert, you always have the right to question things and investigate the facts for yourself. Remember that experts can make mistakes and sometimes different experts will have conflicting opinions. This is one reason people often get a second opinion before undergoing a major medical operation.

Don't base big decisions on big assumptions

You may be thinking that you hear thousands of facts a week. Can you really be expected to check all of them just to be sure you don't make any poor assumptions? And I agree with this sentiment. We have to be practical. Take into account whether the information is really important anyway. If there is a trivial fact that makes no influence on your life, then you don't need to look it up since it is not important. But if you find yourself about to make a big decision based on a "fact" you have only heard from one source, stop yourself and try to verify the fact from at least one more reputable source first. It is possible that this act will save you from making a critical mistake. When making big decisions, if at all possible avoid basing them on big assumptions.

Test your assumptions

Again, we all make assumptions, but we should test them occasionally. Here is an example. Although it may seem simple, it is illustrative of how you could test your own assumptions. Take the equation $1 + 1 = 2$. It is an equation, which gives it an extra authority, so there is no need to question it, right? Well, let's do it anyway for the sake of an example. Imagine this. You take one marble and another marble. You put them together and you get two. Then you take one apple and another apple. You put them together and you also get two. Then you take one glass of orange juice and another glass of orange juice. You put them side by side, and you also have two. So far the equation works perfectly. But then you decide to add the orange juices together by pouring one glass into the other. Now you have a glass with double the orange juice, and one empty glass. Apparently, 1 glass of orange juice + 1 glass of orange juice can sometimes just result in one even fuller glass of orange juice. Test your assumptions and you may find other interesting exceptions like this. (Of course, if we were to have measured just the volume, it would have doubled, perhaps from 100 mL + 100 mL = 200 mL)

As a fun fact, Alfred Whitehead and Bertrand Russel spent 360 pages in *Principia Mathematica* (not to be confused with Isaac Newton's book) proving that 1 + 1 = 2. Although Kurt Gödel later refuted some key assumptions that were made in the work. Many of us might assume that the business of proving simple math operations would be simple, but philosophers and mathematicians have shown this to be more complex than it might appear.

Secret Principle #19: **Objectivity**

Look at Problems and Situations Objectively

"Genius is simply the completest objectivity, i.e., the objective tendency of the mind.... Genius is the power of leaving one's own interest, wishes and aims entirely out of sight, of entirely renouncing one's own personality for a time, so as to remain pure knowing subject, [and gain a] clear vision of the world."

— **Arthur Schopenhauer**, German philosopher.

Geniuses Who Applied the Principle

Aristotle, René Descartes, Albert Einstein, Temple Grandin, Abraham Maslow, Arthur Schopenhauer, Socrates.

Description of the Principle

The ability to be objective is not something that will come naturally to most of us. By the nature of our existence, we are subjective creatures because we have a specific perspective. We have eyes and senses that give us information about ourselves and the things that immediately surround us. It is very difficult for us to see things as they truly are. Instead, we naturally tend to focus on how everything relates back to us. But to be objective means to look at situations as a detached observer. It means to remove the want or the need to get a specific result. When you desire something, your desire will make you expect a certain result, and you will be more likely to overlook problems. Being motivated can be good, but too much passion can actually color your perception and lead you away from being objective.

For objectivity, it is important to lose the self. Usually, the most objective response is to find the best outcome for everyone involved. If you are too concerned with how everything affects you personally, you won't be able to be objective. This doesn't mean that personally, you don't matter. It just means other people matter too. But being objective can actually get more complicated and difficult. For example, humans affect the lives of other animals. Someone who is truly objective would probably take into account other life forms, and what effect their actions have on them as well.

Perfect objectivity is probably not attainable in most situations. But if you are able to take into account how your actions affect more people than just yourself, or more groups than just your own, then you will be more objective than most people. And you will be much more likely to make better decisions overall.

Benefits of the Principle

The objective person will be in a much better position to make the best overall decisions. Someone who is highly objective will make a great leader. No one wants a leader who is only interested in his or her own benefit. However, a leader who can take into account how big decisions influence many people will be highly valued. Consider the CEO of a large company. In his decisions, he shouldn't just consider what choices will raise his paycheck alone. He should consider how his actions can influence employees, other leaders in the organization, clients, investors, and many of us would say the environment too.

Being objective is useful for understanding a problem or situation as it actually is. Instead of getting too caught up in one part of a problem, or in how the problem affects you personally, you will be better able to perceive the full extent of it. A good understanding of problems, in an objective way, is a clear marker for the genius mind. In their ability to see a problem as it is, they are often the ones in the best position to make progress in solving it.

Consider this story reported in *The 50th Law* by Robert Greene and 50 Cent, about the hip hop artist Curtis Jackson (a.k.a. "50 Cent"). First, keep in mind that his beginnings were in a very rough neighborhood, where the main options in life were to work a minimum wage job, or sell drugs. The first would lead to poverty, the second would likely lead to jail time and exposure to violence. In his youth, he chose a life of dealing drugs. A powerful moment for him was when he came across the principle of objectivity, of seeing things as they truly are. This principle would change his life forever:

> One day ["50 Cent"] was discussing the troublesome aspects of the game [e.g., dealing drugs] with an older hustler named Truth, who told him something he would never forget. Don't complain about the difficult circumstances, he said. In fact, the hard life of these streets is a blessing if you know what you're doing. Because it is such a dangerous world, a hustler has to focus intensely on what's going on around him. He has to get a feel for the streets—who's trouble, where there might be some new opportunity. He has to see through all the bullshit people throw at him—their games, their lousy ideas. He has to look

at himself, see his own limitations and stupidity. All
of this sharpens the eye to a razor's edge, making him
a keen observer of everything. That's his power.

You might think that of course objectivity and seeing things
as they are is important in such tough environments, but it
doesn't matter as much elsewhere. But this assumption would
be wrong. For 50 Cent, he found it even more important to
remain objective as he rose to stardom in the hip hop world.
For instance, executives could be ruthless. A musical artist
could be popular one year, and gone the next. Seeing the likely
pitfalls of relying too much on a musical career, he claimed
his stake in a variety of ventures. These have included work
as: a businessperson, actor, investor, film producer, rapper,
entrepreneur, and screenwriter. This is a benefit of objectivity,
of seeing things as they are. You see more than your peers, and
so you are prepared to take the most beneficial course of action.

How to Apply the Principle

Learn some cognitive biases

You may have heard about cognitive biases. They are thinking
errors that people often make. It is important to be aware of
them, because they usually present us with inaccurate views of
the world, and should be taken into consideration if we want to
be fully objective. You will find it useful to familiarize yourself
with some of them, in your efforts to think more objectively.
Wikipedia has a large list (e.g., search "List of cognitive biases").
Here are a few examples:

- **Confirmation bias** — the tendency to search for or
  interpret information in a way that confirms one's prior
  expectations.

- **Dunning-Kruger effect** — the tendency for unskilled individuals to overestimate their own ability and the tendency for experts to underestimate their own ability.

- **Reactance** — the urge to do the opposite of what someone wants you to do out of a need to resist a perceived attempt to constrain your freedom of choice.

Learn some logical fallacies

Logical fallacies are errors people make in their logical reasoning. Being unable to see a situation in a logical way, of course makes us less objective. If you can, it would also be helpful to learn more about logic in general. But logical fallacies can be especially helpful to study because they show us the most common types of mistakes that people tend to make in their reasoning. You will find it useful to familiarize yourself with some of them, in your efforts to think more objectively. Wikipedia has a large list of them (e.g., search "List of fallacies"). Here are a few examples:

- **Appeal to emotion** – where an argument is made due to the manipulation of emotions, rather than the use of valid reasoning.

- **Circular reasoning** (circulus in demonstrando) – when the reasoner begins with what he or she is trying to end up with; sometimes called assuming the conclusion.

- **Red herring** – argument given in response to another argument, which is irrelevant and draws attention away from the subject of argument.

Imagine yourself as an objective robot or alien

Imagine yourself not as a human, but as a robot, programmed to assess situations and problems in a neutral way. Or you can imagine yourself as an intelligent alien from another planet, and you have just arrived to earth, seeing everything with fresh eyes. Try to assess situations and problems in such a removed way. Interpret everything new you see as something strange and remarkable. Allow yourself to forget that these are familiar things you see every day. This can take practice to become good at, but you should find that your ability to accurately perceive situations and problems should improve with time.

Withhold judgment

Don't feel the need to come to a firm conclusion on everything right away. We are often quick to judge situations on very little information. This can be adaptive because it helps us continue to move forward rather than stay still. But consider that movement isn't always progress. Often, different people will have wildly different explanations and viewpoints of the same thing. Take the time to consider all the possibilities, and all the different explanations of events. Make sure to consider evidence and actions above words when possible. Words lack objectivity. They can be used to state one event in an infinite amount of ways. The same event can be stated negatively or positively, for example. Also, words can be abused, and used to lie or completely misrepresent something. Actions, although sometimes ambiguous, are often more clear than words.

Also consider when there are many viewpoints available to you, that perhaps there is no one correct way to view the situation. There may be more evidence to believe one scenario over another, but objectively, you may not have access to the definitive and final truth.

Secret Principle #20: **Simplify**

Simplify; Take the Complex and Boil it Down to its Essence

"Everything should be made as simple as possible, but not simpler."

— **Albert Einstein,** German-born theoretical physicist.

Geniuses Who Applied the Principle

Albert Einstein, Martin Luther King, Jr., John von Neumann, Orville and Wilbur Wright.

Description of the Principle

Be cautious with ideas worded in very complicated ways that are too difficult to understand. It is easy to think when something is described in an overcomplicated way that it must be an excellent idea. You may assume the author of the idea is more intelligent than you, and therefore you must trust what they say. However, sometimes ideas are phrased in too complicated of a way. This may be either because the person isn't skilled enough to phrase it more simply, or more worrisome is that they may want to mislead you, to try to sound more credible than they actually are.

As simple as it may seem, it is not necessarily a simple exercise to keep your ideas and messages simple. For example, if you are asked to write down what you did last summer, this should be easy if you are given two pages. But what if you are only given four sentences? Many of us would start to have trouble at that point, and need to carefully think about the most important things we did, and state them in the most direct and concise way. Simplicity isn't always easily accomplished, but brilliant minds tend to find a way to make things simple so the information can be understood and applied more efficiently.

Benefits of the Principle

The ability to make things simple can help you prove to yourself that you truly understand something. If someone wants to tell you about a large complicated topic, and they can explain in detail how everything works, then they must have a good understanding of the topic. But a test of whether they truly have a higher level understanding is if they can break it all down for you in a more simple way. Remember what Albert Einstein said: "If you can't explain it to a six year old, you don't understand it yourself."

Another key benefit of keeping things simple is that it will be easier for you to give clear explanations. Perhaps you have subordinates, colleagues, or even friends who you would like to explain a difficult topic to. It will be very helpful then to be able to take what you do, or your topic of interest, and describe it simply. Understand that people who work outside of your field or area of expertise will not know many technical details or the terminology that may be common to your area. Because of this, they are more likely to get lost if you make your explanations too complicated. Keeping things simple will help get your ideas across more directly.

Here is perhaps the biggest benefit. We live in a world where most of us want to reach the greatest amount of people. Whether you have a product to sell, a message to spread, or an issue to raise awareness to, most of us want to reach more people. Well, when you get used to describing things in a simple way that most people would understand, you will allow yourself to reach the biggest audience that you can. One of the reasons Dr. Martin Luther King Jr.'s "I have a dream" speech was so effective is because it was something many people related to. But the other key reason is because it was stated directly, in a simple way everyone could understand. If he had used much bigger words that no one could relate to, his message wouldn't have reached as many people or left such an impact.

How to Apply the Principle

Summarize your work processes

When you complete a project, practice summarizing it down to its simplest parts, either in your mind or on paper. Often, we perform tasks and complete projects without fully processing what we have done. We just complete one task and move on to the next. To be sure that you understand what you are doing, and have actually learned something, take ten minutes and summarize your process and what you learned. Keep things simple. This will be especially useful if you attempt to do this without referring to your notes first. If your boss or a respected colleague asks you without warning to explain your project simply, you don't want to be seen flipping through notes, do you?

Explain something technical to a novice

If you want to be completely sure that you are keeping things simple, in an effective way, get some help from someone who knows very little about your field or projects. For example, you may explain it to your grandmother or to a child until they can understand it. Even though it may be frustrating to do this with someone who isn't familiar with your work, it can be very helpful. You may get asked numerous questions, but this is good. It will force you to be sure that you understand all of the basics. And sometimes, the non-experts ask interesting questions that would not occur to actual experts in the field. These can help give you something new to think about, and strengthen any weaknesses in your understanding.

Secret Principle #21: **Define**

Define Problems Clearly

"There's no sense in being precise when you don't even know what you're talking about."

— **John von Neumann,** Hungarian-American pure and applied mathematician, physicist, inventor, computer scientist, and polymath.

Geniuses Who Applied the Principle

Albert Einstein, Galileo Galilei, Ernst Mach, John von Neumann.

Description of the Principle

You might ask why defining the problem is important. It's important because having a very clear grasp of a problem is what you need in order to solve it effectively.

Often, when we are faced with a problem, we want to solve it and get it out of the way as soon as possible. Because of this, we may jump right in and attempt to work on it, without having put any real thought into what the problem actually is.

Instead, the best approach is to define exactly what the problem is. It's easy to become overconfident that you know what to do, but before you jump in, ask yourself what the goal is. What is the final thing that you are trying to accomplish? And why is it important to do?

In fact, defining the problem is largely about knowing what types of questions to ask. For example, these should help:

- What is the problem?

- What caused this problem?

- Is this a problem that I could solve?

- Is this the real problem, or is there an even bigger problem that is causing this one?

- If I ignore this problem, will it resolve itself naturally?

- What would the solution to this problem look like?

Keep in mind that in order to solve a problem, you may find that you need certain tools, resources, or even that you need experts to answer some of your questions. Either way, it is powerful to first define the problem so you can figure out the best path that will lead you to the solution.

Benefits of the Principle

By defining problems you can save yourself time and be more effective at solving it. Computer programming, for example, is something that can take a great deal of thought and work to code something properly. A programmer who doesn't carefully think about the problem, and just jumps in will probably end up with a mess of code. Worse yet, later on he may be unable to make sense of the code or even to get it to work. He will probably realize that he hadn't properly defined what the problem even was. If he had thought through it to begin with, he would have saved time and been more productive.

Let's consider Albert Einstein. When asked what he would do if he had an hour to save the world, he said: "I would spend 55 minutes to understand and formulate the problem, and 5 minutes to come up with ideas/execute the solution." In other words, he would define exactly what the problem is. The example of needing to save the world may seem silly, but you can easily imagine some other great problem that needs to be solved. What is the response of most people? The main responses may be to either become overwhelmed, or to react immediately without much thought. An immediate reaction will likely be an automatic type of response that doesn't fully consider the problem. The danger here is that you can make things worse, and cause even bigger problems. Of course, the point here isn't to spend exactly 55 minutes defining a problem, and five minutes executing the solution. The point is to make sure you understand a problem thoroughly before you begin trying solutions. The bigger the problem, and the more grave the potential consequences, the more important this is.

Trying to solve a problem before you have defined it, for example, can lead you into working on irrelevant issues that don't help you to make progress. Instead, when you define a problem clearly, you will understand it more fully. This will help you think up better potential ways of solving it without going down paths that simply create more problems.

How to Apply the Principle

Ask questions that help you define the problem

As mentioned above, you may try asking some of these questions to help you define a problem:

- What is the problem?

- What caused this problem?

- Is this a problem that I could solve?

- Is this the real problem, or is there an even bigger problem that is causing this one?

- If I ignore this problem, will it resolve itself naturally?

- What would the solution to this problem look like?

If it helps, write down as many responses as you can think up, and take some time to review them before you attempt to solve the problem.

Create an operational definition

Creating an operational definition means to define an exact process. This is the sort of thinking computer programmers may use before turning their thoughts into computer code. For example, let's say a computer programmer creates a robot that can move around, identify objects, and move those objects. You may want to instruct it to make you a peanut butter and jelly sandwich, but the problem is it doesn't understand the concept. You need to operationally define what you mean. So instead, you instruct it to open the refrigerator door, take out the peanut butter, jelly, and bread. Then, to get two slices of bread out, get a knife from the drawer, and spread peanut butter and jelly onto the bread, and so forth. This is the true definition of the problem (for the robot) of making a peanut butter jelly sandwich. The point here is to avoid being vague, and instead to be precise with exactly which steps need to be completed, in what order, and with what materials to get the desired results.

Turn your operational definition into a system

Take the idea of an operational definition one step further. Create protocols, checklists, or procedures so that everyone can be in agreement with how something is defined. This way, they can solve problems using an established system to increase efficiency. There is no reason for you to solve the same exact problem in a different inefficient way each time. Define the problem once very thoroughly, then use the same system that is proven to work each time you have that problem. This technique is especially useful for problems you have to solve regularly.

Find a definition everyone can agree on

If you work in a group or as a team, make sure everyone agrees on the general definition of a process or of a problem. It can be useful to ask everyone how they would define the problem, until you can find points that everyone can agree on. Open discussion can help pinpoint an exact definition, and increase understanding of the problem you are working on.

Secret Principle #22: **Patterns**

Consider the Big Picture and the Overall Patterns

"Look again at that dot. That's here. That's home. That's us. On it everyone you love, everyone you know, everyone you have ever heard of, every human being who ever was, lived out their lives. The aggregate of our joy and suffering, thousands of confident religions, ideologies, and economic doctrines, every hunter and forager, every hero and coward, every creator and destroyer of civilization, every king and peasant, every young couple in love, every mother and father, hopeful child, inventor and explorer, every teacher of morals, every corrupt politician, every 'superstar,' every 'supreme leader,' every saint and sinner in the history of our species lived there – on a mote of dust suspended in a sunbeam."

— **Carl Sagan,** looking at the Earth from the perspective of the vast cosmos, American astronomer, cosmologist, astrophysicist, astrobiologist, author, science popularizer, and science communicator.

Geniuses Who Applied the Principle

Charles Darwin, Albert Einstein, Carl Sagan, Leonardo da Vinci.

Description of the Principle

It's good to know some of the details in your field, and to know them in depth (Principle #12). Obviously, this can help you to make progress in your area. But you must also understand the big picture, the big patterns and trends. For example, if you are a biologist, you may specialize in DNA and genetics, but it is still important to know how the whole biological organism works. You must understand that DNA is in the chromosomes, the chromosomes are in the human cell, cells make up tissues, and tissues make up organs, which make up the human body. This is the big picture overview.

Knowing the big picture allows you to have a general understanding of a large amount of information. This is something that comes with time in studying a field. At first, when starting out, it may be easier for you to focus on details. In fact, you're likely to get lost in those details and not truly understand everything. But geniuses and brilliant minds understand that they need to rise above those details and connect ideas on a larger overview level.

Benefits of the Principle

The benefit of understanding the big picture is that you will have a good general understanding of your subject area. It will be easier, then, for you to build a higher level of understanding off of this general understanding. When you need to learn something at depth, or in detail, you will quickly realize where it fits in with the big picture. Someone without an understanding of the bigger patterns is much more likely to get lost if they continue to simply learn detail after detail. They will lose focus of how everything interconnects.

Also, when you have a broad overall understanding, it is easier to make connections between different fields. For example, someone who has a general understanding of physics, math, and chemistry is likely to see many connections between them and be in a good position to make progress within those fields.

To see a more detailed example of a benefit of looking at the big picture, consider the TV series, *Cosmos: A Spacetime Odyssey*, narrated by Neil deGrasse Tyson (although the original version of *Cosmos* was narrated by Carl Sagan). In the first episode, a cosmic calendar is presented. The point of it is to reveal on a compressed one year calendar, the history of the universe. This allows us to see the big picture in a simple fashion. Keep in mind that the universe is actually about 13.8 billion years old. But when compressed into one year for the sake of our cosmic calendar, we gain a "big picture" perspective.

The calendar shows that the big bang happened January 1st, forming the beginning of the universe. The Milky Way Galaxy formed in May. The Solar System and life formed in September. Photosynthesis started in October, and eukaryotic cells (with a nucleus) arose in November.

We are now almost at the end of the year and humanity hasn't come into existence yet. December 14th we have sponges, on the 17th we have fish, and on the 20th we have land plants. On the 21st there are insects and on the 23rd there are reptiles. On the 25th we have dinosaurs, the 26th we have mammals, and on the 28th we have birds and flowers. On the 30th dinosaurs go extinct and on the 31st (the final day of the year) we have human evolution. At just around noon, finally modern humans arrive. In the last 60 seconds, we have had the most recent ice age, agriculture, civilization, and pretty much every invention that has ever been created (e.g., tools, books, art, technology, etc.).

The benefit of the big picture is that we can make sense of a lot of information in a small space. It is easy to get overwhelmed with too much information to consider, especially in today's world where most of us have access to seemingly unending amounts of information, simply through the internet. This is a principle that allows the greatest amount of understanding in the most efficient way. It will be a powerful way to think, learn, and understand.

How to Apply the Principle

Test your big picture understanding

Take stock of your overall understanding, occasionally. It's easy to assume you know something well if you never test yourself. Even if you are in school or college, doing well on exams isn't always enough to show that you have a full grasp of the big picture. It is a good idea to take notes or draw diagrams of how you perceive everything to interconnect. Even if you feel lost, drawing diagrams or concept maps can help you to head in the right direction. Perhaps you can look up information in books, encyclopedias, or online to figure out the relationship between the many concepts.

Ask a master or expert to explain the big picture

Another way to gain a broad overview is to simply ask a master or expert for help. You might tell them that you are studying a topic, and you understand some details, but you are getting lost in understanding things on an overview level. Experts are in a particularly good position to help explain this for you, with their great experience. Keep in mind that there are different levels of overviews and big pictures. For example, if you are studying plants, you may find an expert and ask about the broadest overview possible. You could ask for a basic overview on how all lifeforms work. They may tell you that DNA, the cell, and reproduction are some of the common themes to all lifeforms. Then you could go a bit deeper, and ask for an overview on how all plant life works. What do all plants have in common? You could also go even deeper still, and ask for an overview for a specific species of plant. Even if you don't know an expert firsthand, you may be able to find one online who is willing to help.

Pay Attention to Anomalies, to Unexpected Events that Seem Accidental

"The exception proves that the rule is wrong. That is the principle of science. If there is an exception to any rule, and if it can be proved by observation, that rule is wrong."

— **Richard Feynman,** American theoretical physicist.

Geniuses Who Applied the Principle

Marie Curie, Thomas Edison, Richard Feynman, Alexander Fleming, Johannes Gutenberg, Louis Pasteur, Wilhelm Rontgen.

Description of the Principle

An anomaly is something that does not fit the normal or expected pattern. As human beings, we are great at finding and understanding patterns. In fact, as quick as computers can process, and as "smart" as they have become, one of the ways the human brain is far superior, is in that of pattern recognition. For example, Yohan John, who has a PhD in Cognitive and Neural Systems from Boston University, considered this question in the *Forbes* article, "How powerful is the brain compared to a computer?" Part of his response included:

> *Humans are spectacular at several things, including pattern recognition, language abilities, and creative thinking. Computers are rapidly improving at pattern recognition, but most programs still don't do as well as children. A classic example of pattern recognition is face recognition. We are capable of recognizing faces in a variety of contexts. We can even recognize faces that have aged, or are disguised, or are obscured by facial hair. Computers are not nearly as good as humans at such tasks.*

As you can see, we tend to recognize patterns fairly quickly, especially in familiar environments and situations we are used to. However, sometimes there is an anomaly, or an exception, which is something that stands out as being different. The anomaly is a challenge because how can we make sense of something that is unfamiliar? Unfortunately, since we don't make sense of such things quickly, we tend to ignore them, therefore failing to take them into account. We also may assume that the anomaly is a mistake. We may think there is nothing useful in it, and that it could be a chance circumstance, a coincidence. However, anomalies can be much more than this.

As an example of the importance of anomalies, consider Alexander Fleming. He is the man who discovered the benefits of penicillin. He was not looking for a cure to anything at the time. Fleming was actually studying the properties of staphylococci, which is a type of bacteria. During his research, he noticed some mold (later identified as *Penicillium notatum*) had contaminated his bacteria cultures. On close examination, he was surprised to see that the mold appeared to have killed some of the bacteria.

This was an anomaly. Remember, Alexander Fleming's research wasn't concerned with what may cause bacteria to die. Another scientist might have simply said "This is kind of interesting, but it's not what I am researching," and moved on. However, Alexander Fleming realized that if something was killing the bacteria, this may be an important finding. Luckily, he and other researchers investigated it further, and ultimately realized the powers of penicillin to cure various illnesses.

To show you the grim situation before Fleming's discovery, here is what Dr. Oz has said on Biography.com about the pre-antibiotic or pre-penicillin world:

> Imagine a world before antibiotics. This is a world where a papercut to your finger could result in amputation, where mothers feared for the wellness of their children. It was a world where bacteria were beating mankind.

And to show you the power of anomalies, here is what Dr. Ali Khan (also on Biography.com) has said about the discovery:

> Antibiotics are one of the greatest breakthroughs of man. They have saved hundreds of millions (of billions) of lives since they were first identified in the early 1900s.

Clearly, this was one of the greatest breakthroughs in medical science, and the discovery has saved a countless number of lives.

Some of us may be tempted to put all of our focus on the anomalies. They are interesting and fascinating, so who cares about broad patterns... Why not just jump straight into studying the exceptions to the patterns so we can all make breakthroughs? I can relate to this, as I have always been drawn to the exceptions, the abnormal, and the mysterious. However, we must first understand the broad patterns in a field. In understanding the big picture and the typical patterns, you will be better able to identify an anomaly when you see one. The big picture is key to your general understanding, and the anomalies are key to making progress in a field. But they both work together. You cannot understand one without the other.

Benefits of the Principle

As seen in the example above with Alexander Fleming and penicillin, being alert and aware of anomalies can help position us to make great discoveries. Often, however, we are in a rush to get the results we expect. We can become so focused on one thing that we fail to realize that an anomaly is important, and could change everything. We must avoid becoming closed off to outside possibilities, and avoid becoming fixated on just one outcome. Instead, we should pay attention to unexpected discoveries, and increase our chances of making a big breakthrough. Ultimately, this open-minded approach can help us to have a breakthrough in our understanding, scientifically, or in our field.

Looking for and understanding anomalies can help turn you from an expert into a true master of your domain. Many people are capable of quickly becoming aware of trends and patterns in a field. But it takes much greater depth of curiosity and understanding to learn the many exceptions to the rule. To learn the rules, without knowing the exceptions can even have dangerous or disastrous effects. For example, consider an airline pilot. You wouldn't want to take a flight with a pilot who was only prepared for routine and normal events. Of course, we expect him to have that competency. But we would also want him to know how to handle a wide range of unexpected or anomalous things that might happen. A simple thing airlines do is they always have two pilots working. For one to get sick or be unable to work would be unusual, but they are still prepared for that possibility. Airlines understand the importance of being prepared for anomalies. The benefit in this case is that it saves lives.

Paying attention to anomalies can also help your creativity. Remember that people often neglect anomalies, thinking that they are chance events with little meaning. Being aware of and observing such unusual occurrences can help with your creative ability. For instance, one way to be creative is to consider unusual or unexpected forms of information. This is what anomalies are. When you are able to connect unusual bits of information together, you will be able to generate more unique, original, and interesting ideas.

How to Apply the Principle

Don't assume an unexpected result is a mistake

When you get an unexpected result or byproduct, do not assume it was just a meaningless accident. Try the same process again and see if you still get the same unexpected result. If it happens again, don't assume it was an error. Of course, you have to consider that maybe you did make a mistake somewhere. But be careful in how you define mistakes. In Alexander Fleming's experiment, it was a "mistake" that his bacteria was dying. He probably didn't protect it well enough. But of course, it wasn't really a mistake, it was an anomaly that revolutionized medicine as we know it. Don't define everything as a mistake too quickly. Just because the result was not what you intended to happen, does not make it a mistake. Consider if the unintended effects could be in some way useful, even to someone in a different field. Could it have some greater meaning? Discuss the possibility with colleagues or even people outside your line of work. Sometimes a different point of view can be helpful to realize the potential benefits of an anomaly.

Document and record anomalous findings

When something anomalous happens, document it. Even if it seems like a complete accident, or like it is irrelevant, write it down. It is easy to think in the moment that it isn't important, but later on you may forget exactly how you achieved a certain outcome. Always keep in mind that it is easy to misunderstand or overlook the implications of an anomaly. You will want to have documentation of everything you did to get your unusual results.

Brainstorm about the implications of an anomaly

When you witness an anomaly, consider if it resulted in something positive or negative. Was this something you would want to happen more often, or something awful that you never want to happen again? In either case, it will be important to study the anomaly and understand it better, so you can either make it happen again, or prevent it from ever happening again. Ignoring it, or acting as if it is a coincidence will not accomplish anything.

Secret Principle #24: **Analysis**

Calculate and Analyze

"The general who wins the battle makes many calculations in his temple before the battle is fought. The general who loses makes but few calculations beforehand."

— **Sun Tzu,** Chinese general, military strategist, and philosopher.

Geniuses Who Applied the Principle

Bobby Fischer, Stephen Hawking, Miyamoto Musashi, John von Neumann, Sun Tzu.

Description of the Principle

This principle can apply broadly to competitions, warfare, strategy games, as well as real life scenarios. To paraphrase Sun Tzu above, the one who calculates further, and goes in with a plan and preparation, is much more likely to succeed in the end. The reason Sun Tzu's message is so powerful is because it is true both on the battlefield and off of it.

The principle is not difficult to understand. Consider

someone who is at any competition, who uses no strategy, and who always goes directly for the objective with no regard for how to handle the obstacles that are on that path. This person is likely to lose. The one who considers all of the obstacles and engages in calculation and planning to circumvent them will tend to prosper, and prosper greatly against the one who does not even have a plan.

As often is the case, this principle will center on knowing what type of questions to ask. For example:

- What is the biggest problem I am facing and that needs immediate attention?

- What can I do to stop the progress of my competition? Is there a way I can mislead my competition (such as to make them think I am strong when I am weak, or vice versa)?

- For the actions I am planning, what are the most likely reactions or consequences? Are any of those consequences likely to cause me more problems?

- Where is the best place for me to position myself, or my subordinates, to produce the biggest effect? (for example, in *The Art of War*, Sun Tzu recommended to position oneself above the enemy in battle, such as on a hill to gain an advantage)

- How deeply have I, my colleagues, or competition thought through the problem? (Hint: a principle of chess is to think one move deeper than you think you need to. You will find it useful to do the same in your real life problems to avoid surprises).

Of course, these questions may be a bit broad for your specific goals. But you should be able to adapt them to a wide range of situations and problems.

Benefits of the Principle

As Sun Tzu said, those who analyze more deeply will win. For most people, this is a good enough benefit. When you calculate further, you will perceive further, and see further into the future possibilities than those around you. You will have the advantage. Someone who didn't calculate will be blindsided, surprised by every commonplace obstacle that comes their way. Failure targets the unprepared, whereas success targets the well prepared.

As we all know, sometimes it is more important to work together as a team, and sometimes it is more important to focus on undermining the competition. This principle can apply in both cases. For example, in today's world we often work in teams. If you have a team or group that you help with your analytical abilities, the principle may be viewed as collaborative and competitive all at once. By analyzing deeply, you would be able to help your team and hurt the competition at the same time. When used in this way, the principle can be especially powerful.

Keep in mind that calculating and analyzing is not easy work. Many of us avoid it because it takes a great deal of mental energy. For example, how many times have you heard someone say "I'm not very good at math"? People are often weak at calculating and analysis, because they specifically avoid doing it as a matter of habit. But if you can train yourself to become good at it, you will likely become indispensable. If your analyses lead to accurate predictions and successful outcomes, whoever you are working with will never let you go.

If you think this is a skill which only applies to chess or warfare, or obscure areas, that is not the case. The skill of calculating, analysis, and ultimately judgment can transfer broadly to other areas. For instance, you may find it interesting that some top chess players have turned to working as expert Wall Street investors and analysts.

Consider Boaz Weinstein, a Chess Master who manages a hedge fund and also has a reported net worth of 450 million dollars. Clearly, it isn't possible for Weinstein to calculate every single possibility in chess or with stocks. But this is the same situation we are all faced with in daily life problems. Although to Weinstein's credit, he was able to transfer his calculating abilities from the board, over to analyzing stocks and predicting which ones will perform better than expected. Keep in mind that the skill of calculating and analysis can apply as widely as you are willing to take it.

How to Apply the Principle

Fight through the mental fatigue

Calculating, by nature, requires mental work and effort. Many of us may prefer to take action than to sit and think through every possibility. Mental fatigue can set in rather quickly, and rather than calculate, the easier option seems to be to make a quick judgment call, even if we have not carefully analyzed every option available to us, and the potential consequences. This can be a disastrous mistake. Sun Tzu would remind you that in the battlefield, it will cost many lives. You must understand when you are in a serious situation, and keep in mind that a hasty ill-thought decision will have consequences. The effort and mental strain you put up front will be worth the rewards you receive later on. Likewise, the quick action with little thought will not be worth the grave consequences that may come later.

Train the body to strengthen the mind

As offbeat as it may sound, you may choose to train physically to help keep your mental stamina up. This will help you to be able to calculate as long as necessary to come to a correct solution. Bobby Fischer, former world chess champion, was sometimes laughed at for his response to how he trained for a chess tournament. He claimed, on the *Dick Cavett Show* in 1971, that a big part of his training was physical. He liked to run and swim, but he claimed it was to keep in top physical shape to play chess. After the laughter subsided, he explained that to sit still for four to five hours at a tournament actually required a lot of stamina. To have the mental focus to make good chess moves for that long is not easy. Apparently, his peak physical conditioning helped him to stay in peak mental condition, which helped him make deep calculations, great moves, and win the World Chess Championship in 1972.

You may be interested to learn that researchers have found a strong link between exercise and brain functioning. For example, here is an excerpt of an article by *Harvard Health*, "Regular exercise changes the brain to improve memory, thinking skills":

> *Exercise helps memory and thinking through both direct and indirect means. The benefits of exercise come directly from its ability to reduce insulin resistance, reduce inflammation, and stimulate the release of growth factors—chemicals in the brain that affect the health of brain cells, the growth of new blood vessels in the brain, and even the abundance and survival of new brain cells.*

The evidence shows that adding an exercise routine to your schedule could help promote intellectual abilities, or to help keep them from declining.

Follow through on planning and taking action based on your calculations

As you analyze problems and situations, you will sometimes find that there is great potential for disaster. You will foresee a big danger that could happen. You can't be certain that it will happen, but you can't take the risk, because if it does then it would ruin all of your plans. When you notice these dangers, these cracks that you don't want to fall in, you must form contingency plans, or what we often call backup plans. It is foolish not to calculate at all. But perhaps the only thing more foolish is to calculate, and then not prepare for the dangers you have identified. If you notice big potential issues, you must form plans, or backup plans to deal with them if they should arise.

Do a post-mortem analysis

Every day, thousands of students will receive grades back from a big exam. Some will get A's, but many will get B's, C's, or worse. The interesting thing is that many of those students who did not receive an A, will glance at their grade and put it away. They know the grade, so this is all that matters, right? They can't change the grade now, so it only seems practical to forget about it. Actually, after a failure, or even results which were not quite the best, this is the perfect time to do a post-mortem analysis. This means to analyze any mistakes that were made, and how you could have done better. Of course, this is the least likely time most people will want to analyze, because they are tired of the material. But in fact, it can be the greatest learning experience. Do the post- mortem analysis while the task is still fresh in your mind. Do not wait too long. It will be especially helpful to ask someone more knowledgeable than yourself to help. This applies to any project, not just school grades.

Secret Principle #25: **Analogy**

Think in Terms of Analogies

"Growth comes through analogy, through seeing how things connect, rather than only seeing how they might be different."

— **Albert Einstein,** German-born theoretical physicist.

Geniuses Who Applied the Principle

Charles Darwin, Albert Einstein, Galileo Galilei, Isaac Newton.

Description of the Principle

You are probably already aware of what an analogy is. It is simply a comparison between two things that are alike in some way. They can often be especially helpful for understanding something new. When trying to make sense of something new and unfamiliar, people often have no point of reference to understand something, so it is important that they be able to build a connection with a topic that they are already familiar with. However, analogies are not only useful with learning about new areas. They can also be useful to understand a known topic in a different or deeper way.

As an example of an analogy, one I have heard is that human bodies are like cars. If one part of the car fails, the whole system will often fail to work. And it is the same with a human body. If one organ fails, the whole system will often fail to work properly. But keep in mind that analogies are not meant to work perfectly. They often don't. The point is to quickly build an understanding of how different topics relate. If you do look for exceptions or loopholes in analogies, you will probably find them, and that is okay. They still serve their purpose. In the human – car analogy, for example, human bodies are obviously different than cars. A human body is capable of healing and self-repair to a certain extent, and a car is not. Humans are alive, and cars are not. Also, for either humans or cars, it isn't always the case that when one thing fails, the whole system will fail. For example, the human body can function without an appendix, and a car can still function with broken tail lights.

Benefits of the Principle

Albert Einstein used an analogy to help explain a difficult idea, relativity. He said: "Put your hand on a hot stove for a minute, and it seems like an hour. Sit with a pretty girl for an hour, and it seems like a minute. That's relativity." This was a brilliant comparison, because Einstein is usually seen as working on the most difficult problems in physics, and believed to do work most of us would not expect to fully understand. Yet he managed to explain relativity in a very simple way. Of course, his analogy will not fully explain the phenomenon, but for someone who is new to understanding relativity, his short explanation can be a lot more meaningful than a weighty and thoroughly explained academic text would be.

When you need to explain something in the simplest way, for a child or for someone who works outside of your field, analogies can be one of the best ways to do so. Keep in mind that many people either cannot handle all of the details involved in a difficult problem, or they are simply uninterested in them. An analogy can be a powerful way to concisely explain how something generally works. It is short, simple, and most importantly, highly effective.

Analogies work very well with keeping things simple (Principle #20). Using good analogies is about finding the ones that are simple and effective. This is useful not just for explaining things to others, but also to help you understand your own field, or related topics, in a new way. Analogies can help you to build up unique connections, and ultimately a greater understanding.

How to Apply the Principle

Think beyond your industry to find interesting analogies

Practice thinking about how aspects of your field relate to other industries. But don't limit yourself to thinking just of other *work* industries. Allow yourself to explore entirely new directions. Let your thoughts drift into thinking of nature, the planets and stars, movies you've seen, and so forth. Do not limit yourself, and you may discover some interesting analogies that help advance your understanding of your own field. Many of us think we understand everything we need to know about our work and our expertise. But if you seek unique and interesting analogies, you may find that your perspective of your work shifts entirely.

Make something easier to understand

If you frequently have trouble explaining a topic to people, this is an excellent time to search for analogies that may be helpful. In fact, you could try telling a story that is based on an analogy. For example, an editor might explain what he does to a construction worker this way:

> *You know when you've finished your construction work, but there is still a mess? There are still random materials lying around that don't belong, like sawdust, maybe half drunk soda bottles, and other junk. Someone needs to go back and clean up the excess junk that isn't needed, to make sure the final work is well-polished and presentable. That is what I do as an editor for writers.*

When you break down a new topic by comparing it to a much more familiar one, you will make it much easier for people to understand your message.

Secret Principle #26: **Perspective**

Take Multiple Perspectives; There is Seldom One Right Way

"I believe everyone should have a broader picture of how the universe operates and our place in it. It is a basic human desire. And it also puts our worries in perspective."

— **Stephen Hawking,** English theoretical physicist, cosmologist, author and Director of Research at the Centre for Theoretical Cosmology within the University of Cambridge.

Geniuses Who Applied the Principle

Walt Disney, Henry Ford, Stephen Hawking, Arthur Schopenhauer.

Description of the Principle

Consider the default perspective that you will have for your full life. Naturally, it will always be the perspective that comes from your own body, through your eyes, ears, nose, mouth, skin, and thoughts. It is normal to consider everything from this perspective. Thoughts that you may have as a result are

"Am I hungry? Am I tired? What do I want to do today? Do my co-workers like me?" and so forth. Obviously, many of the thoughts we have will revolve around ourselves, which only makes sense, given that this is the main perspective we have.

However, this principle is really about gaining a wider perspective. It is about considering multiple viewpoints, and gaining a more accurate picture of a problem or situation. You may take into account the viewpoints of other people, for example, or even different ways to view a problem. Imagine if everyone thought the same way and used the same perspective. Some problems would be very difficult if not impossible to solve. Instead, we need to be open to perceiving a problem in different ways.

Benefits of the Principle

We often get locked into one perspective. We get used to thinking in one way all of the time, and so it becomes an old habit, and it can become increasingly difficult to perceive reality in a different way. But when you do extend beyond this, and start to open up your point of view, you will start to perceive something much closer to reality. Keep in mind that the reality of a situation isn't usually based in a single perception. Instead, it is often based on taking into account as many perspectives as possible. The more perspectives you can understand, the better you will be at forming a full picture of a problem in your mind.

When you expand your ability to see multiple viewpoints, you will also be able to deepen your understanding of humanity. Sometimes, we are quick to judge others, but when we truly make an effort to understand different viewpoints and perspectives, we will tend to become less judgmental and more receptive to other ways of thinking and viewing the world. In this greater understanding, you are much more likely to become a better communicator, more persuasive, and more diplomatic.

These are qualities good in themselves, but also good for getting results. If all you can do is antagonize people, and try to convince them that they are wrong and you are right, you will not make progress. Progress is made through understanding the perspective of others, and communicating to them in a way that takes their perspective into account.

As an example, consider the famous Indian parable (translated by John Godfrey Saxe) about six blind men who are presented with an elephant. But never having seen one, they do not know what it is. So they begin to feel it in different places.

"Hey, the elephant is a pillar," said the first man who touched his leg. "Oh, no! It is like a rope," said the second man who touched the tail.

"Oh, no! It is like a thick branch of a tree," said the third man who touched the trunk of the elephant.

"It is like a big hand fan" said the fourth man who touched the ear of the elephant. "It is like a huge wall," said the fifth man who touched the belly of the elephant. "It is like a solid pipe," Said the sixth man who touched the tusk of the elephant.

The men began to argue with each other about what the elephant was, when a wise man passed and told them that they were all correct. But actually, it was all one creature and they had all felt a different part of it. The blind men understood then, and stopped arguing.

Often, we have an understanding of something, and we are completely sure of ourselves. The reason to expand perspectives isn't because we are wrong. But sometimes, there are many correct perspectives, and in order to gain the most full and accurate picture, we have to consider those different viewpoints.

How to Apply the Principle

Consider different types of perspective

One way to shift perspective is to keep in mind many different perspective types that you can take into consideration. Here are some examples of different systems you can think through to expand your perspective. Macro (big) versus micro (small). Personal versus public. Economic motives versus philanthropic motives. Time periods (medieval, renaissance, modern, etc.) or in terms of cultures or locations (Asia, Europe, America, etc.).

Take someone else's point of view

Whenever you find yourself in disagreement with someone, do your best to consider things from their point of view. You don't need to accept their point of view as your own, but try to understand how someone with their upbringing and understanding of the world could come to the perspective that they have. Try to justify their actions and imagine how perhaps even you would have taken their viewpoint if you had had similar experiences as them.

For example, go as deeply as you can into their past. Don't settle for a superficial understanding of the person. What generation were they a part of? Did something very dramatic happen in those times, like a war or an economic crisis? What type of people did they grow up with? What was the general attitude or opinion of the people they were surrounded by? What did their parents do for a living? What kind of income did they have? What was the general environment like? Was it well kept, or run down? Did they face any special difficulties that might have changed the way they saw the world? (e.g., a disability, poverty, prejudice, etc.) When you have gone as deep as you can, ask yourself, if everything had happened to you exactly as it did for them, would you feel the same as they do? Is your perspective right and their perspective wrong? Or are they simply just different perspectives, not necessarily right or wrong? Think about the questions and your answers deeply. Don't rush to a conclusion.

Seek alternative viewpoints, even when you are extremely firm on where you stand

When you have a viewpoint that you know you are especially firm on and that you are certain you would never change your position on, it is still helpful to consider the alternative viewpoint. Chances are you already understand what you believe, and that you know your position very well. Interestingly, many of us choose to surround ourselves with people, books, and messages that *support* our own worldview. However, we could stand to learn a lot more if we sought out information and perspectives that *opposed* our worldview. This can feel extremely uncomfortable for some people. It will mean if you are a democrat, to sometimes listen to news networks who side more with republicans (or vice versa). It will mean if you are atheist, to occasionally listen to the experiences and beliefs of religious people (or vice versa). The extra challenge is not just to expose yourself to other viewpoints but to actually take them in with an open mind. Again, the point is not to change your mind, but to simply expand your ability to understand how and why others may perceive the world in a different way.

Learn a new language to practice shifting perspectives

Even if you do not become fluent, learning a new language can be a useful exercise. Speaking another language is a great way to start perceiving the world in a new light. Many things will be different from what you are used to, forcing you to consider a different perspective. For example, how words are arranged into sentences, the use of certain types of phrases, and the culture will probably all be different from what you are used to. All of these things will expose you to a new way of seeing the world. If you learn enough, you may become interested in traveling to a country where your foreign language of choice is spoken. When you do speak with people in their native language, they will see that you are open to perceiving the world in a different way, and you may be surprised that they open up to you and show you a different way of thinking, doing, and being.

Secret Principle #27: **Intuition**

Develop Your Intuition

"Your time is limited, so don't waste it living someone else's life. Don't be trapped by dogma – which is living with the results of other people's thinking. Don't let the noise of others' opinions drown out your own inner voice. And most important, have the courage to follow your heart and intuition."

— **Steve Jobs,** American information technology entrepreneur and inventor, co-founder and former CEO of Apple.

Geniuses Who Applied the Principle

Albert Einstein, Bobby Fischer, Jane Goodall, Steve Jobs, Stu "The Kid" Ungar.

Description of the Principle

I used to think intuition was a word that didn't have much practical use or meaning. But I was wrong. According to Merriam-Webster, "intuition is a natural ability or power that makes it possible to know something without any proof or evidence: a feeling that guides a person to act a certain way without fully understanding why." In other words, intuition is about having a higher level understanding. It is what happens when you attain a high enough level of expertise that you seem to know automatically what needs to be done in a given situation in your field. You will perform the necessary actions, but may not be able to explain well what you have done, why you did it, or even why it ended up being the correct thing to do. To the novice, intuition may appear magical, like a trick, or perhaps blind luck. But it is the furthest thing from this. Intuition is the result of much practice and forming a true understanding.

Consider Bobby Fischer, one of the greatest chess players of all time. He understood chess so deeply that he did not need to think through every possible chess move to know if it was any good. This played to his advantage in blitz games (or speed chess), where he was known to dominate despite having very little time to calculate moves. Instead of calculating, he had an intuitive feeling as to whether one path would be better than others. He could quickly focus his attention on the one or two worthwhile paths due to his intuition, instead of needing to waste time and energy on a lot of paths that would lead to a losing game. Fischer was able to understand positions quite deeply in very little time. Some people may confuse intuition for making fast calculations, but this is not how it works. Intuitive powers allow one, through great experience, to understand a problem well enough to know the likely conclusions without needing to think logically step by step through every detail.

There are various jobs or fields where powers of intuition are greatly important. For example, some people make a living tapping watermelons, to check if they are ripe and good to eat. Others check newborn chicks to determine the gender. As reported in "The Art of Chicken Sexing" by Richard Horsey:

> *Expert chick sexers are able to quickly and reliably determine the sex of day-old chicks on the basis*

of very subtle perceptual cues. They claim that in many cases they have no idea how they make their decisions. They just look at the rear end of a chick, and 'see' that it is either male or female.

You might wonder why anyone would want to determine the sex of a newborn chick in the first place. The answer is economics. To farmers, the more valuable chicks are the females, because they will lay eggs which can be sold. Therefore, they would prefer to invest their time and money on raising these females. And they prefer to identify them soon after birth, as opposed to spending energy on raising too many males which will not lay eggs.

There are also professional poker players who do not focus on the math of the game. Rather, they are experienced enough that their intuitive grasp makes it unnecessary to do deep calculations. Consider Stu "The Kid" Ungar, widely believed to be the best poker player who ever lived. He was also so good at Jim Rummy that most players refused to play him. And he won so much at Blackjack that he was eventually unable to find a game in Las Vegas. Stu Ungar, and players like him, develop a feel for how they should play their hand. This is based on the thousands of hands they've played in the past and seen others play.

In *Your Worst Poker Enemy* by Alan N. Schoonmaker, he summarizes how intuition can work:

The intuitive players have a gift, and it is as natural to them as Michael Jordan's miraculous moves were to him. When someone unexpectedly blocked him, he responded instantly by switching hands, twisting his body, and shooting the ball a little higher with a little different spin. He could never tell you how he did it; it was just by feel or instinct.

Some great poker players have that gift: they remember how you played a certain hand or they see a look in your eye or they sense something from the way you handle your chips, and they make exactly the right play. If you ask why they did it, they probably can't say. It just felt right.

I think of intuition as a developed instinct. It is not a true instinct, because by definition, instincts are innate, not learned. But intuition is a developed sense that becomes an automatic process (like an instinct). This intuitive feel helps us bypass the need for deep calculations, even when dealing with complex problems.

Benefits of the Principle

Intuition is not an ability we can choose to turn on and off. It is built up over time with expertise in an area. But when you do build up your levels of intuition, the benefits can be immense. To some people, you may even appear to have a special power, as silly as this may seem. You will be able to do things that astound people and seem impossible, simply through a highly developed sense of intuition. The key benefit is that you will be able to make precise decisions that lead to the best outcomes in a short time, and have great confidence in your abilities.

Someone with highly developed intuitive abilities can be extremely productive, and highly valued. Often, the intuitive person will be able to see things that escape others. One of the keys to achieving the highest levels of productivity is to develop intuitive skills, as this will help solve tough problems in a faster more efficient way. Understand that intuition is a higher level skill set, and there are many people who will never fully develop this ability. An intuitive ability will be expressed differently in different fields. But in certain fields, as with watermelon checkers (for ripeness) and chicken sexing, intuition will clearly have very direct and immediate benefits.

How to Apply the Principle

Gain expertise first

There is no simple shortcut to reach a high level of intuition. To develop it will require a great amount of work, probably over a long period, and to become an expert in a field. Even expertise alone may not be enough to fully develop your intuitive abilities. To develop the highest level of intuition will usually require ongoing practice using it as a skill. But it is pointless to try to exercise your intuition until you have at least some expertise in your field or topic.

Understand that intuition will be a different type of skill in different domains. An intuition for knowing what people are feeling will be a different type of skill than an intuition for composing music. You will have to focus on one kind of intuition at a time in order to master it.

Practice your intuition

A way to help develop your intuition when you have built your expertise, is to practice making intuitive judgments, of course. Many of us never practice intuition, probably because we are not aware that it is a skill that can be practiced. But it can be. As an example, consider reading people's feelings as an intuitive skill. When you walk into your work area, or your classroom if you are a student, you can try studying the faces of some of your colleagues. Try to figure out if they are sad, happy, tired, content, upset, disappointed, proud, etc. When you think you have the feeling pinned down, you can simply ask how their day is going, and see if their response lines up with the feeling you detected in them. If you think this is a flawed way to test your intuition because someone can lie, or appear happy but be sad inside, this is true. There is a lot of potential deception in human behavior, and I would say taking those things into account is part of strengthening your intuition. The other point I would make is that intuition is not easy to test for, and every way to test and develop your intuition will probably have some flaw. This is one of the reasons few people develop their intuition to a high level, because it is not simple or easy to make progress with it. It will take true dedication and work.

Verbalize, or write down the things you do intuitively (or without thought)

Many of us are intuitive at something. If you have a child, perhaps you know what all of her facial expressions mean automatically, without being able to put it into words. If you look at the sky on a cloudy day, perhaps you sense whether it will rain or not. Intuitive feelings are difficult to put into words, and it may feel like an impossible task at first. But simply practicing breaking it down into concrete steps, may help you to learn new things more intuitively.

Here are some key questions you can ask, which may help in breaking down your intuitive processes:

- What is the most important feature (e.g., signal, clue) that helped me get to the correct solution?

- Where did my mind go first, when I came across this problem?

- What are the actions I take, every time I have this problem? And in what order do I do them?

- Are there certain key things I always observe or check, before I am able to solve the problem?

- What seems to cause others failure, but allows me to succeed at this problem?

The point of thinking through such questions is to help you get into a habit of breaking down the thought process or action steps that you go through in solving problems intuitively. This will give you a better insight into how intuition works, which may help you to actually learn to be more intuitive in other areas.

Secret Principle #28: **Freedom**

Maximize Your Freedom of Action and Limit the Constraints

"Intelligence should be viewed as a physical process that tries to maximize future freedom of action and avoid constraints in its own future."

— **Alex Wissner-Gross,** American computer scientist, inventor, and entrepreneur.

Geniuses Who Applied the Principle

Jorge Luis Borges, Albert Einstein, Alex Wissner-Gross, John Locke, John Stuart Mill, Artificial Intelligence Systems.

Description of the Principle

Alex Wissner-Gross, the computer scientist quoted above, has researched the importance of freedom of action for artificial intelligence (AI) systems. Even though he mainly applies the principle to AI, he believes this is one of the most universal properties of intelligence. He gave a fascinating TED Talk called *A New Equation for Intelligence* (viewable at TED.com) on the topic.

The key point of this principle is that a truly intelligent person, system, or entity will desire to maximize its personal freedom to act. This means it will want to maximize its freedom to make choices, so that in the future it can continue to have many choices or options to make. To understand why this principle is important, consider that the one thing we can be certain of in life and the universe, is uncertainty. And this uncertainty exists because everything around us is constantly changing. Sometimes it happens in a minor way that is barely noticeable, and sometimes in a major way that can be unsettling. A way to help us make the best decisions, no matter how things change, is to pursue the freedom we need to always make the best choices. Keep in mind that another way to view this principle is that we want to limit the constraints placed on us. We want to reduce or eliminate anything that restricts our options.

The implication of this principle is that an intelligent system or person will be thinking ahead. It will be trying to judge whether certain actions it can take will increase its freedom of action. And it will also try to judge whether certain actions by others will reduce its own freedom of action. This principle is mentioned toward the end of this book because really this implies many things. It implies the necessity of good senses to take in information (Principle #1), having a strong foundation or breadth of knowledge (Principle #11), being objective and seeing things as they are (Principle #19), and understanding the big patterns (Principle #22). It appears that when many other principles are put in place, this one emerges. This is in effect a sort of mega-principle, and one we should all pay attention to.

Benefits of the Principle

When you increase your freedom to act, and eliminate possible restrictions on your ability to act, you will be more adaptive (Principle #3). You will allow yourself the most options, and therefore have the greatest opportunities available to you. If you think of the human being as compared to other animals, a key difference is that we are capable of handling a wider variety of problems. Most animals are masters of one or a few skills or abilities. The bloodhound has its sense of smell. The cheetah has its speed. The tortoise has its protective shell. Although humans do not innately have these abilities, we are not as limited. For example, humans train bloodhounds to track the scents that are important to us. We build vehicles to go faster than a cheetah. And we have created a variety of protective gear that suit more situations than a protective shell would, often allowing for much greater flexibility.

We are always capable of learning and mastering something new. A key benefit of increasing our freedom of action is that the more freedom we have, the more options we have, meaning we have a higher ability to make good choices. For example, imagine that someone much bigger and stronger than you picks a fight with you, and keeps walking toward you until there is nothing between you and him. And you are stuck in the corner of a room. You have made the mistake of allowing him to restrict your freedom of action. Your options are now severely limited, and your opponent has every advantage. With such few options, it is much more difficult to engage in intelligent behavior. It would have been more intelligent to have taken any action necessary to avoid this restriction.

When you increase your freedom of action, you will release yourself from many limitations. You will be in a better position to solve creative problems because of this. For example, the concept of "thinking outside the box" is really about exploring beyond your traditional ways of thinking. We often confine ourselves to certain expectations, but if you increase your range of freedom and see outside of those expectations, you will find that some problems, especially creative problems that seem unsolvable, can suddenly be approached. Many creative problems are set in a way where people tend to define the problems more narrowly than they really are, for example. Looking beyond those limitations will improve your ability to solve them.

How to Apply the Principle

Keep control over important resources

Keep as much control as you can over the major resources in your life. For example: time, money, important material and resources for your field, your personal health, etc. Be cautious how these things are cared for, used, and spent, because these resources are incredibly important. For example, if you don't use your time appropriately, then you won't have the freedom or control to make good choices. If you spent your money on unnecessary things, again you may lose your freedom of action, unable to pay for the things you truly need. Rather than being able to take a job you like for slightly less pay, you may feel forced to take a higher paying job you dislike because you have immense debts that need to be paid.

Increase your own freedom of action, and restrict the opponent's

When you are in a competition where only one side can win, you should consider ways to improve your own freedom of action, and ways to restrict the opponent's freedom of action. You can also add constraints for them to deal with. In battle, one example of adding restrictions to your enemy would be to control their sources of food and water, which would cause their army to fall apart, thus winning without bloodshed. As reported at Romanmilitary.net:

> The Romans realized that with the training a soldier requires, his food, his armor, his armaments, his salary, and his honorarium (paid to those who received honorable discharges), a soldier was a very expensive proposition, and was far too valuable a resource to waste. Therefore, the best tactic would be the one that had the most effect without exposing the troops to unnecessary risk. Their answer was to cut off their opponent from his resources. Armies run on their stomachs and equipment, and both require regular supplies. Without a steady supply of food and water, an army will starve or dehydrate, killing or demoralizing the troops. Eventually, the army would fall apart.

For the curious, the Romans accomplished this in one of three ways. They would attack the resources themselves, interrupt the supplies en route, or initiate a siege (e.g., surrounding and attacking the city).

Notice that such actions by the Romans or other armies could have two major effects. It increases the freedom of the friendly forces, giving them energy and resources to gain strength (if they manage to get a hold of the resources themselves), and it reduces the freedom of the forces they are invading, because they will have less supplies and resources to live off of.

You probably aren't at war. But to apply the concept in your own life, you can re-envision a competition or game you are involved with. Then, make your goal to increase your freedom of movement and options, and to restrict the freedom and options of your opponents. This can apply to one on one physical competitions like wrestling, to larger team competitions like with soccer, or even with playing board games such as chess, checkers, risk, or monopoly, etc.

Secret Principle #29: **Problem**

Focus on a Big Problem, or a Network of Related Problems

"Concentrate all your thoughts upon the work at hand. The sun's rays do not burn until brought to a focus."

— **Alexander Graham Bell,** scientist, inventor, engineer and innovator who is credited with patenting the first practical telephone.

Geniuses Who Applied the Principle

Albert Einstein, Johann Wolfgang von Goethe, John von Neumann, Isaac Newton.

Description of the Principle

The most brilliant minds tend to identify a big problem that they want to tackle, and then they move forward on trying to solve it with all of their intellectual strength. Of course, sometimes when you have a very large problem, there are actually many smaller problems that must be solved along the way to the big one. Whether you focus on one very large problem, or prefer to focus on smaller problems that are interrelated, the point is that you will have a firm focus in one area.

Even if you study a given field, this principle doesn't simply mean to study problems within that one field. It goes deeper than this. It means to focus on problems that are related in some way. For example, an archaeologist who studies ancient cultures may choose to research them based on geography. If he chooses to focus on cultures in Central and South America, for example, he may choose to study the Aztecs, Mayans, and Incans. This would be simpler and more effective than jumping around to different continents to study different unrelated cultures.

Notice that despite this principle, some of the geniuses mentioned in this book have been greatly accomplished in a variety of fields (e.g., Leonardo da Vinci, Johann Wolfgang von Goethe). However, for the majority, they chose to focus mostly on one area, or a network of related areas. For example, a writer may have written novels, as well as short stories and possibly some poetry or screenwriting. A filmmaker will tend to focus on related skill sets such as directing, producing, editing films, and possibly photography. A scientist may be well versed in chemistry, physics, mathematics, and some biology.

Consider John von Neumann, a man who contributed to a great amount of fields, such as physics, computer science, statistics, and economics. But when you look at the fields he worked in, we can see a pattern. All of the areas he pursued were related in some way to mathematics. He was a man of numbers, symbols, and equations. He focused entirely on a network of related problems that dealt with math.

Benefits of the Principle

The benefit of focusing on problems that are interrelated is you will be able to learn more efficiently. Even if you study mathematics and you decide that you want to expand, you will be much more efficient in your progress if you decide to branch out into physics and computer science, as opposed to if you choose to branch out into botany and sculpture, for example. To go into related domains will still take work and learning, but you will have the core knowledge base which will help you learn new things more easily. You won't have the disadvantage of someone who has no knowledge of the topic whatsoever. Of course, when you do branch out too far (e.g., from botany to sculpture), you will start out again as a complete novice. Your knowledge of botany will provide little help to you, unless of course you decide to sculpt plants.

If you decide that you want to resist this principle, and use Leonardo da Vinci, the most famous Renaissance man, as an example, realize that he was not satisfied to stay on the surfaces of a new area. He immersed himself deeply into everything new that he undertook. He didn't dabble in art, science, and engineering. Instead, he took the time to master them all. If you choose the path of da Vinci, realize that it will take great persistence to achieve mastery in multiple and unrelated areas. Although this is an honorable path, it is not the advised one. It is difficult enough to achieve mastery in one area, and to promote yourself as being more worthy than others with similar skills. The world today is hypercompetitive, and so it isn't good enough to be good. You have to be great. Those with a complete focus have the advantage in achieving greatness.

Another benefit is that this is probably the most efficient path toward genius. Let's take a big picture overview of some of the names mentioned in this book thus far. Even at age 16, Albert Einstein was gazing into a mirror, wondering what it would look like if he were traveling the speed of light. He

worked at a patent office for many years because it allowed
him the freedom to focus on his work in physics problems.
Even on the days up to his death, he was focused on making
progress with his unified field theory. Bobby Fischer's life, from
the age of six, was essentially all about chess. If you weren't
playing or talking about chess, he wasn't concerned with it.
Prince played 27 instruments on his debut album, For You. His
life revolved around his music. All of them had profound focus
on a key area. For Einstein, it was physics, for Fischer, chess,
and for Prince, music. Most brilliant geniuses in this book, or
elsewhere, have followed a similar pattern.

How to Apply the Principle

Master one field at a time

Tackle one subject at a time. Make sure you fully understand
what you are doing before you move on to another topic. This
can take great patience. It can take years. Many people are
inclined to get bored, and will jump back and forth between
different fields, but the way to make a lasting masterful impact
in a domain is to focus completely in one area. Some people
want to quantify the time or effort required. They may say it
takes ten years, or 10,000 hours, or something else. But there
isn't necessarily one point where you wake up and you are an
expert. Also the time and effort required will vary from person
to person, and from field to field. It probably takes longer
to master quantum physics than it does to master the art of
juggling.

Commit to one project at a time

Avoid abandoning projects midway. Commit to finishing and learning something from your endeavors. Often, we want to quit because a task is difficult and we feel unprepared. But if we push through and finish a task, we are in a position to take our learning to a higher level. It is obviously a huge commitment, to do what many of the most brilliant minds have done and focus on one key area for a majority of one's life. But it is a big start to stay focused on one project to its completion. You will severely limit your ability to learn and grow if you consistently quit when a task becomes difficult. This is actually the time when it is most important to push through, to keep going despite the challenge. Remember that surely many geniuses had doubts and wanted to quit, but they chose to keep on going anyway. If they can do it you can too. Don't expect to be a star when you try something new. It takes time.

Concluding Thoughts

"The fool doth think he is wise, but the wise man knows himself to be a fool."

— **William Shakespeare,** English poet, playwright, and actor.

Stay Humble

I want to tell you a story about the importance of humility.

I saw a video the other day where a man was being harassed by two others. It was late at night. There was no one else around. The lone man insisted that he did not want to fight, and he told the other two to go away. They approached him, closer and closer. The lone man stood tall, put his hands out front ready to fight since there seemed no way out. When one of the aggressors got too close, the lone man easily dodged attacks and managed to get some solid punches in. Shaken up, the two aggressors backed up a bit, but they still would not leave. The lone man warned them that they needed to leave or he would hurt them seriously. He said, "I'm not joking." The two men didn't seem to care, and the fight continued. The two men lunged forward, but the lone man was too quick at avoiding the attacks, and he hit them in return once again. At one point, the lone man even grabbed a Dolly (e.g., a metal tool used to carry furniture), and he used it as a weapon, and also to protect himself. The two aggressors became more cautious and backed up a bit, but they would not leave. Eventually, the police did arrive to arrest the two men who started the fight.

The lone man clearly knew how to fight and take care of himself, but he was humble. He didn't want to fight anyone. He didn't feel the need to show his superiority over others. Most of all, it seemed that he didn't want to hurt anyone. As I watched the video, I was under the impression that the lone man could have killed these two men if he had truly desired it. But he only injured them to protect himself. He never hurt them anymore than he needed to.

A similar analogy can hold for the intellect. Someone who has just come upon these secrets principles may want to show superiority over others. Perhaps someone could even be tempted to bully people intellectually. But you should know that the truly brilliant minds in history did not behave this way. They were aware that there is always more to learn, more to understand, and more progress to make. They also understood that everyone starts somewhere. To be temporarily ignorant is acceptable as long as you have the desire to learn. So if you want to brag, brag about how much progress you've made over where you used to be. But there is no need to compare yourself so much with others.

I have been lucky. I have had the luxury to always have my needs taken care of so I could focus on bettering my mind. Not everyone is this fortunate, and I do not look down on anyone for it.

Rather, if I can help you to learn and apply these principles, which you may never have otherwise had access to, then I am happy to do so.

Essentially, I am saying that it is important for us to use *The Secret Principles of Genius* for good. Use your intellectual energy to improve yourself, to solve your own problems, a friend's problem, problems at work, or even to focus on larger world issues. This is infinitely more important than appearing to be more intelligent than someone else.

Bringing it All Together

Very briefly, this section will establish how all of the principles can work together to help you in your journey to meet your genius potential.

In the first section of *The Secret Principles of Genius*, we learned the importance of personal qualities. For instance, pay attention to your senses (Principle #1), as this is the way your brain receives all of its information which it then interprets. It is also vital to keep your curiosity or to reawaken it (Principle #2). Never lose this, because it is the spark of the genius mind. It is the starter in your vehicle that propels you forward on the road to genius. Without that spark, your mind cannot take you anywhere. Also, you must persevere (Principle #8). Train yourself to keep moving forward even when obstacles come your way. Do not back down at the first sign of trouble. Those who achieved great intellectual accomplishments fought through great struggles as well. It wasn't easy for them, so don't expect it to be easy for yourself. Always have the highest standards for yourself and your work (Principle #7). Genius isn't born in mediocrity, but through a desire to meet the highest level of quality possible. Ultimately, you will have to put in the work (Principle #9). Even the most accomplished geniuses of the world were not able to create their ideas, inventions, and works of art through thought alone. The reason we remember the most brilliant people is often because they put a gifted mind to work diligently so we could bear the fruits of their labor.

In the second section of the book, we discovered the importance of learning. A genius mind cannot get anywhere without some level of knowledge. First, work on your core foundation (Principle #11). Learn the things that are important for every educated citizen to know. Understand basic math, science, history, geography, language skills, the classics, and so forth. When your core knowledge and skills are well developed, you are ready to start building expertise in one area that interests you the most (Principle #12). You can pour your energy into this. But it will always be useful to have knowledge in other areas too. Put some of your time into learning new things happening in other areas. For the brilliant mind, learning is critically important. A good way to be sure that you are truly learning and digesting the information is to take notes and look back on them periodically (Principle #13). Also, recall that you don't have to go alone on your journey. Many masters before you have walked a similar path, and you can learn immensely from them (Principle #14). Ultimately, it will pay off to turn learning into something that happens as a normal part of your life. This is the way of the genius.

In the third section, we learned the importance of using key strategies for thinking and problem- solving. One of the core tools of a genius mind is to remain as objective as possible (Principle #19). They conduct a search for the truth by trying to forget about their own desires, or their own wishes for a certain outcome. Great minds like Albert Einstein also emphasized the importance of keeping things simple (Principle #20). You should be able to explain your big ideas even to a child. This will help to communicate your ideas, but also to make sure that you fully understand everything about them. It is also important to think about and understand the big patterns in your field (Principle #22). Know the general expectations and trends, and then it will be much easier for you to identify anomalies. Anomalies are the things that do not fit into the expected pattern (Principle #23).

Pay special attention to anomalies, as they are often ignored, misunderstood, or assumed to be errors. In fact, they can lead to a big breakthrough, as has happened often throughout history. One of the most important principles appears to emerge as we apply other principles in the book. This is the principle of increasing your freedom of action. All intelligent entities (e.g., from humans, to animals, to robots) will keep their own level of freedom as high as possible, while restricting the freedom of any opponents (Principle #28). And finally, the surest path to genius is to focus on one big key problem, or a network of interrelated problems (Principle #29). This is the path that the majority of geniuses have taken for millennia.

The secret principles of genius all work together in some way, which is what makes them powerful. For them to be useful to you, you will need to put them into action. I would recommend choosing two or three from each section of the book and starting with those. It can be overwhelming to attempt to apply them all at once. But if you apply a few to begin with, you will be able to start on your path toward genius right away.

The path that was once blocked, has been opened. Now there is nothing holding you back from reaching your genius potential.

Thank You

Thank you for taking the time to read *The Secret Principles of Genius*. I hope that you found the information useful. Just remember that a key part of the learning process is putting what you read into practice.

Before you go, I want to invite you to pick up your free copy of *Step Up Your Learning: Free Tools to Learn Almost Anything*. All you have to do is type it in your browser: mentalmax.net/EN

Also, if you have any questions, comments, or feedback about this book, you can send me a message and I'll get back to you as soon as possible. Please put the title of the book you are commenting on in the subject line. My email address is:

ic.robledo@mentalmax.net

Did You Learn Something New?

If you found value in this book, please review it on Amazon so I can stay focused on writing more great books. Even a short one or two sentences would be helpful.

Support I. C. Robledo by Writing A Review Here:

mentalmax.net/SPrev

Did You Learn Something New?

An Invitation to the "Master Your Mind" Community (on Facebook)

I founded a community where we can share advice or tips on our journey to mastering the mind. Whether you want to be a better learner, improve your creativity, get focused, or work on other such goals, this will be a place to find helpful information and a supportive network. I hope you join us and commit to taking your mind to a higher level.

mentalmax.net/FB

JAICO PUBLISHING HOUSE
Elevate Your Life. Transform Your World.

ESTABLISHED IN 1946, Jaico Publishing House is home to world-transforming authors such as Sri Sri Paramahansa Yogananda, Osho, The Dalai Lama, Sri Sri Ravi Shankar, Sadhguru, Robin Sharma, Deepak Chopra, Jack Canfield, Eknath Easwaran, Devdutt Pattanaik, Khushwant Singh, John Maxwell, Brian Tracy and Stephen Hawking.

Our late founder Mr. Jaman Shah first established Jaico as a book distribution company. Sensing that independence was around the corner, he aptly named his company Jaico ('Jai' means victory in Hindi). In order to service the significant demand for affordable books in a developing nation, Mr. Shah initiated Jaico's own publications. Jaico was India's first publisher of paperback books in the English language.

While self-help, religion and philosophy, mind/body/spirit, and business titles form the cornerstone of our non-fiction list, we publish an exciting range of travel, current affairs, biography, and popular science books as well. Our renewed focus on popular fiction is evident in our new titles by a host of fresh young talent from India and abroad. Jaico's recently established Translations Division translates selected English content into nine regional languages.

In addition to being a publisher and distributor of its own titles, Jaico is a major national distributor of books of leading international and Indian publishers. With its headquarters in Mumbai, Jaico has branches and sales offices in Ahmedabad, Bangalore, Bhopal, Chennai, Delhi, Hyderabad, Kolkata and Lucknow.

SINCE 1946